Haynes

Desktop
Publishing
Manual

© Haynes Publishing 2006

Published by: Haynes Publishing
Sparkford, Yeovil, Somerset BA22 7JJ, UK
Tel: 01963 442030 Fax: 01963 440001
Int. tel: +44 1963 442030 Fax: +44 1963 440001
E-mail: sales@haynes.co.uk
Website: www.haynes.co.uk

British Library Cataloguing in Publication Data:
A catalogue record for this book is available from the British Library

ISBN 1 84425 3171

Printed in Britain by J. H. Haynes & Co. Ltd., Sparkford

Throughout this book, trademarked names are used. Rather than put a
trademark symbol after every occurrence of a trademarked name, we use
the names in an editorial fashion only, and to the benefit of the trademark
owner, with no intention of infringement of the trademark. Where such
designations appear in this book, they have been printed with initial caps.

Whilst we at J. H. Haynes & Co. Ltd. strive to ensure the accuracy and
completeness of the information in this book, it is provided entirely at the
risk of the user. Neither the company nor the author can accept liability
for any errors, omissions or damage resulting therefrom. In particular,
users should be aware that component and accessory manufacturers, and
software providers, can change specifications without notice, thus
appropriate professional advice should always be sought.

Haynes

Desktop
Publishing
Manual

Kyle MacRae

Contents

Introduction

The difference between an effective and an ineffective publication, be it a letterhead, an advert, a newspaper, a book or even a web page, is that one is read and the other is ignored. The trick is pulling together words and images on the page in a way that grabs and maintains the viewer's attention – and doing so without resorting to cheap tricks and garish gimmicks. In this book, we explain the basics of good layout and design and show you how to produce professional quality projects every time using only your computer.

Tool for the job

Ah yes, the computer. Desktop publishing, or DTP, is the business of using a computer with the appropriate software to create documents ready for commercial or home printing. It sounds a lot more daunting than it is. Indeed, one of computing's best kept secrets is the ease with which anybody can produce professional-looking printed material. All you need is a little know-how, a little imagination and this book. Whether you go freehand or start with a template, the end result should be – *will* be – every bit as good as if you'd commissioned it out to a commercial design house or print bureau.

The book is split into five main sections. Part 1 explores the hardware and software that you'll need, including a good-quality printer. Part 2 introduces the basics of DTP and the principles and practice of effective design. You will learn and develop the background knowledge and hands-on skills required to tackle DTP with gusto. Part 3 takes a step-by-step approach to producing a variety of projects, including business stationery, commercial advertising and a web page. Part 4 deals with

printing issues, including colour separation and submitting work to a print bureau. Finally, Part 5 introduces some enlightening design tips and case studies.

You'll find that we strongly recommend using 'proper' DTP software rather than a word processor or an image editor. If you've ever tried to cobble together a publication using text boxes in Microsoft Word, you'll understand its limitations only too well. However, a dedicated DTP program needn't cost you a fortune. We concentrate on Microsoft Publisher 2003, which comes bundled with some versions of Microsoft Office or can be picked up as a stand-alone program from the likes of Amazon for around £160 (further details on p.17–25). When you factor in what DIY DTP can save you in design and print charges, that's a price well worth paying. As ever, though, it really doesn't matter which program you use, as everything we cover here can be adapted to suit just about any software.

So have fun, be bold (but not too bold) and soon you'll be producing print-perfect designs with the best of them.

DTP on a PC is as easy as 1-2-3.

PART **1**

Hardware and software

PART ① PC versus Mac

Desktop publishing was born in 1985, and it first saw the light of day on the Apple Mac computer. At that time, although Windows had been announced it was not yet on the market, and programs written for IBM-style PCs were essentially text-based, so it was natural that the first desktop-publishing program should be written for a computer that already had a graphical operating system.

That program was PageMaker, and it was produced by a company called Aldus. For the Apple Mac it was to be the 'killer app'; in other words, it was an application so desirable that people would buy Apple's very expensive hardware just to be able to run it. And the hardware was expensive, with a suitably equipped Mac and a LaserWriter printer costing almost US$10,000.

Apple's early lead

A version of PageMaker for the PC was introduced in 1986, but by then Apple dominated the market and nobody who'd invested in a Mac system was going to switch to the PC just because Windows had arrived. At that time, Windows was in its infancy and was completely unproven as a graphical operating system. Very few PCs were capable of running Windows and few people had been tempted to buy it. Early versions of PageMaker had to be supplied with something called a runtime version of Windows in the same box. This was a stripped-down version of Microsoft's fledgling operating system that was capable of running PageMaker, but didn't offer any of the other benefits of Windows such as cutting and pasting between programs.

In 1990, Windows had reached its spotty adolescence in the form of Windows 3.0, but by then a Mac-only program called QuarkXpress had taken over from PageMaker as the preferred software for professional publishers so, even though ten million Windows users were now able to run PageMaker properly, PC users were still effectively sidelined from joining the mainstream desktop-publishing community.

The first Windows version of QuarkXpress appeared in 1992, which theoretically made it possible for Windows PCs to compete

PageMaker's original logo has iconic status in the world of desktop publishing. It's from a drawing of Aldus Manutius, the pioneering fifteenth-century Italian publisher from whom the Aldus company took its name.

A Power Mac G5 with dual processors and up to 800GB of disk storage is ideal for desktop publishing. The cinema-style monitor also allows facing pages of a publication to be displayed side-by-side.

with Macs in the world of desktop publishing, but it was not that simple. The Mac and PC disk formats were not compatible, and there were differences in the way the two versions of QuarkXpress saved their files. In any case, many of the operators involved in desktop publishing were not computer experts and had only been trained to use Macs. As far as they were concerned they weren't using computers at all, they were using desktop publishing equipment. They didn't want to learn how to use a PC and there was no logical reason why their employers should cast aside a significant investment in Mac hardware – and bear the financial burden of retraining staff – just because Windows was becoming the world's dominant graphical operating system.

It's hard to find a new PC that hasn't got what it takes to cope with desktop publishing. What makes this Evesham Quest particularly suitable is the grand scale of its magnificent LCD monitor.

The PC fights back

The average PC of today is as graphically capable, powerful and easy-to-use as any Mac and, given that PCs vastly outnumber Macs, it's not surprising that desktop publishing is a popular application for many PC users. The leading desktop-publishing software titles are available in both Mac and PC formats, so there's no reason to prefer one type of machine over the other in terms of its commercial desktop-publishing capabilities. For home and office use, there are several inexpensive Windows-only programs that offer a low-cost introduction to the fascinating world of desktop publishing.

For historical reasons, the Mac is still deeply entrenched in most commercial print and publishing organisations, so if you're thinking of setting up business in this field the Mac platform is obviously the way to go. But for everybody else, which includes non-professional designers, businesses, charities, clubs, societies and other organisations and individuals who wish to produce professional-looking printed material with the minimum of expense, the Windows PC platform has a number of advantages. Not only are Windows PCs cheaper to buy, there is also a wider range of software titles and hardware add-ons available for them, which makes them more suitable for all-round computing tasks. The Mac is relatively poorly served in comparison and, perhaps because of the Mac's niche status and the fact that many of its users don't have to pay for their own equipment, software and accessories for the Mac still tend to cost more than their PC equivalents.

Problems of compatibility between Macs and PCs are almost a thing of the past. File formats are irrelevant when work can be delivered to a commercial printer over the internet or sent on a standard CD-ROM and, with most commercial printers accepting PostScript and portable document format (PDF) files, which can be produced equally well by Macs and PCs, the hardware and software used to generate the file is immaterial.

The same holds true for desktop publishing projects which are not destined for commercial printing. Desktop-publishing systems are increasingly being used to produce websites, electronically-readable PDF files and a range of materials destined to be printed on local inkjet or laser printers. In all these cases, the choice of computer hardware is irrelevant. The only time it really becomes an issue is when a publication is being worked on as a team project; then it is definitely preferable for each member of the team to use the same software and hardware. In other cases, the choice of hardware will be determined by what's already available or driven by personal preference.

At a pinch you can tackle desktop publishing on a portable PC, but the restricted screen dimensions and the limited input and output options make them far from ideal, however attractive they look.

PART 1 System requirements

Apart from software, which is covered later in this section, there are three essentials for a desktop-publishing system:

- A computer that can run specialist desktop-publishing software and to which additional equipment can be attached.
- Peripheral hardware including scanners, printers and storage drives.
- Ancillary equipment and services such as a broadband internet connection and a digital camera for taking original images.

What to look for in a computer

At the heart of every desktop computer is a system unit. This is the large box containing all the electronics and storage devices, and the rest of the system is connected to it either wirelessly or by cables. The two primary input devices are a mouse and a keyboard, through which you tell the computer what to do. The primary output device is a monitor on which the computer shows you what is happening.

You'll find many of the same components in a laptop PC but the keyboard, monitor and system unit are all crammed into the same case and the mouse is replaced by another sort of pointing device such as a touch-sensitive pad. Another variation is the all-in-one computer where the system electronics and drives are housed inside the monitor but the keyboard and mouse remain separate. For desktop-publishing work, the best type of computer is one that follows the traditional configuration where everything is separate. This arrangement allows individual components to be upgraded as required, and additional drives and devices to be mounted inside the system unit instead of cluttering up the work area and creating a tangle of wires and power adapters.

Apple's iMac G5 is an attractive all-in-one design available at a reasonable price, but the 17in version is suitable only for casual DTP. There's a 20in model that's more suitable for desktop publishing, but additional drives must be connected externally.

This Hewlett Packard Pavilion M5000 is a superb candidate for desktop-publishing work with a fast processor, plenty of storage, a 21in monitor and wireless input devices to reduce desktop clutter.

Regardless of external appearance, what every computer has in common is a set of key components whose suitability for desktop publishing can be gauged simply by examining their specifications on paper. This is mainly a numbers game so you don't need to be a technical wizard to choose a suitable PC yourself. It's just a matter of looking up the specifications on a manufacturer's website, in print advertisements or in magazine reviews, and then comparing them with the information in the table below. In each case, the higher the figures quoted in a machine's specification, the more powerful it is likely to be and the faster it will get things done.

Component	Measurement	What does this describe?	Notes
CPU	gigaHertz (GHz)	The speed at which the computer 'thinks'	Not all processor chips work in the same way so you can't accurately compare the speed of an AMD processor such as the Athlon 64 with a Pentium or any other Intel processor. Neither can you directly compare PC processors with Mac processors. However, you can use the GHz speeds of CPUs to compare processors in the same 'family', be it Celeron, Pentium 4, Athlon XP, Athlon 64 or whatever.
Hard disk	gigabytes (GB)	The maximum storage capacity of the disk	Desktop publishing files can be huge, so it's almost impossible to have too much disk space. Don't consider a new computer with less than 100GB of disk storage.
System memory (RAM)	megabytes (MB) or gigabytes (GB)	The amount of memory available for everyday tasks	Computers use RAM as workspace. Having more RAM is like having a bigger desk, enabling you to work on several tasks at the same time. 256MB is the bare minimum, 512MB is better and 1024MB (1GB) is best if you intend to do a lot of photographic work.
Monitor	inches	The diagonal size of the screen	Most computers come with 17in screens, because these represent a good balance between price and performance for everyday use. While a 17in monitor is fine for casual desktop-publishing tasks, serious work demands a larger monitor. Consider 19in or more if you're buying a slim TFT monitor and 21in or more for conventional CRT monitors. In terms of how much of the screen is viewable, a 19in TFT screen is broadly equivalent to a 21in CRT device.
Optical drive	x2 to x52	The speed at which CDs or DVDs can be recorded and played	The speed of an optical drive is less important than the type of drive you choose. It must be a rewritable drive and it should, preferably, be DVD rather than CD, because a DVD disc can store at least six times as much data. Top speed for CD drives is x52, and the current top speed for DVD drives is x16. The faster the drive, the quicker it can copy large files. A rewritable DVD drive can also handle CDs, so you don't need to buy two drives.

The good news is that you don't have to worry too much about precise specifications if you're buying a new computer because every current model is capable of handling desktop publishing with ease, as is every older PC capable of running Windows XP and every Mac capable of running OS X. If you've got a computer that's more than a couple of years old, you'll find the table a useful guide when choosing suitable upgrades such as more RAM, a bigger hard disk or a new monitor.

Printers and scanners

Even if you intend to have your work printed commercially, you'll need a desktop printer for proofing the finished product before sending it away for publication. There's much more information on choosing and using a printer later in this section, starting on page p.27.

If your publications will consist of material produced by other people, you can't expect all your contributors to have digital cameras and word processors, so you'll need a scanner to turn conventionally printed photographs and slides into digital images suitable for use with desktop-publishing software. Coupled with suitable optical character recognition (OCR) software, the same scanner can also turn printed documents into editable electronic text. The OCR process is not foolproof, but even if you have to tidy up after the OCR software has done its best, it's a lot better than retyping everything manually.

You'll need a flatbed scanner with a glass top and a lid. Scanners works very much like photocopiers, but are usually controlled via software on the host PC rather than through buttons on a control panel. To use a scanner, you place the paper original face-down on the glass plate and then wait while a light source with sensors traverses beneath the glass. Instead of getting a copy on paper, as you would with a photocopier, the duplicated material is piped directly to the hard disk of your PC.

Scanners need not be expensive, and for occasional home use you can get by with a £50 slimline scanner that connects to a USB port and picks up its power from the USB port, thus doing away with the necessity for a mains cable and transformer. The quality of a scanner depends on many factors, including the build quality of the hardware and the sophistication of the electronics. There are two things to look for when evaluating a scanner: colour accuracy and resolution. If the colour of a scan is not true to the original, this can usually be fixed in software, but it means more work for you so it's far better to have a scanner that gets things right first time. One indication of colour quality is the number of bits used to store colour information while scanning (24 bits or more is acceptable), but the only way to find out how well a scanner represents colour is to seek out product reviews on the web. In terms of sharpness, it is the optical resolution of a scanner that counts. This is expressed in pixels per inch (ppi) or dots per inch (dpi), and you should look

A combined printer, scanner and copier saves space but is not as flexible as a separate printer and scanner. The main drawback is that any item to be scanned or copied must be completely flat, so scanning books, magazines and small objects is out of the question.

A flatbed scanner fitted with an optional illuminated lid allowing it to scan transparencies and film negatives.

for a true optical resolution of 600ppi or more. Most scanners can do much better than this, with resolutions of 1200 x 2400ppi being typical, but 600ppi is fine for most desktop-publishing work. Higher figures of up to 9600ppi are often quoted but these are not true figures: they are produced by a process called interpolation, which uses software to enhance ordinary scans made at lower resolutions.

Unfortunately, you can't scan slides with an ordinary flatbed scanner but, for certain models of scanner, you can buy a slide adapter. This takes the form of a replacement lid incorporating its own light source that shines through the slide from behind. A slide adapter can cost as much as the scanner itself, and the results are sometimes unsatisfactory because most flatbed scanners have insufficient resolution to make a good job of slides, bearing in mind the tiny image area of a 35mm slide. You'll get superior results from a so-called film scanner, which accepts film strips and colour transparencies and scans them at resolutions of 2700ppi or more. Film scanners are more expensive than flatbed scanners; they are suitable only for slides and films, so you still need a flatbed scanner for paper originals. Unless you expect to handle a lot of transparencies you can get by with a flatbed scanner and have the occasional slide transferred to CD as part of the digital services offered by many high street and online photographic processors.

Digital cameras

Digital cameras now far outsell film cameras, so with any luck you won't often need a scanner, especially if you shoot your own pictures. The resolution of a digital camera is measured in megapixels, with 3 megapixels being the current entry level and 5 megapixels becoming the norm. You don't actually need the highest resolution for desktop publishing, especially as large files are difficult to store and manipulate, but there is an advantage in having 5 megapixel images if you intend to crop parts from larger pictures and want them to remain sharp.

The simple cameras built into palmtops and mobile phones are not really suitable for desktop publishing unless you're producing news stories where any sort of picture is better than nothing. You'll need to spend £100 or more on a separate camera, which should have an optical (not digital) zoom facility and removable memory cards for storing images. It's also convenient to have a memory card reader, costing only a few pounds, to handle the transfer of pictures from memory card to the hard disk of the host PC. Even though it's possible to transfer pictures from a camera via a cable attached to the computer's USB port, this can be fiddly and rapidly drains the batteries in the camera. Many desktop and laptop computers come with built-in memory-card readers, but any machine can be upgraded by buying an external multi-format card reader and plugging it into a spare USB port.

The following table shows the required resolution in megapixels for some common photographic and international

The Coolscan V is a typical medium-cost, high-resolution film scanner from Nikon. The slide-loading mechanism on the front can be removed to make way for a filmstrip loader.

This is the latest model in Canon's PowerShot range. Its 5-megapixel sensor, 3x zoom lens and macro facility for close-up work makes it an ideal all-rounder for use in desktop publishing.

If original digital images will feature strongly in your publications, an SLR camera is ideal. An SLR viewfinder allows for more accurate composition and interchangeable lenses make the camera more versatile. Best of all, faster electronics allow pictures to be taken in quick succession.

paper sizes. Standard quality at 180dpi is fine for snapshots and community newsletters produced on a home printer but serious DTP work requires a resolution of 300dpi. However, as most of the photographs in a publication are likely to be less than half a page in size, a 4-megapixel camera will do the job. If you anticipate shooting full-page advertisements, think again!

Printed size	Standard quality (180dpi)	DTP quality (300dpi)
6 x 4 inches	0.8 megapixels	2.2 megapixels
7 x 5 inches	1.1 megapixels	3.2 megapixels
A5	1.6 megapixels	4.3 megapixels
10 x 8 inches	2.6 megapixels	7.2 megapixels
A4	3.1 megapixels	8.7 megapixels
A3	6.2 megapixels	17.4 megapixels

It's worth remembering that most digital cameras shoot pictures in a 4:3 aspect ratio, which is the same ratio as a computer screen. Standard photographic sizes are based on differing aspect ratios, including 3:2 (6 x 4), 7:5 (7 x 5) and 5:4 (10 x 8), and the pictures in a DTP publication can be cropped to any aspect ratio you like. The table is therefore only a guide, but one you may find useful when choosing your next camera.

Storage devices

Publications are typically stored on the internal hard disk of a PC and saved onto recordable CDs for sending to a printer. If there is insufficient free space on the existing hard disk of your PC, it's a relatively simple matter to add a second drive provided there is space inside the system unit. If there isn't, you can use an external hard drive that plugs into a USB or FireWire port. A USB hard disk is the easiest type of external drive to install and use.

Broadband internet

With a broadband internet connection, you can receive text and pictures for inclusion in publications and you can keep in touch with contributors via e-mail. Broadband is also an acceptable means by which a finished publication can be sent to a commercial print shop, which saves you the hassle of transferring the publication to CD and sending it through the post. The advantages of broadband don't end there, because it turns the internet into a terrific research tool and acts as a means of locating and downloading images for inclusion in publications – and if you're publishing web pages rather than printed documents, a broadband internet connection is the means by which web pages can be uploaded and updated. Of course you can manage without broadband and use a dial-up connection if that's all that's available, but the large file sizes of finished publications and their associated images mean that broadband is a big time saver.

This tiny USB hard disk from LaCie can be popped in your pocket and is an ideal way of taking finished documents to a printer. It stores up to 8GB of data and can be used as a supplementary hard disk for a desktop PC or as a convenient backup device.

PART **1**

Software for desktop publishing

The only essential software for desktop publishing is a page-layout program. Using one of these you can build the framework of a publication, fill its pages with text and pictures, and then manipulate the layout until it looks exactly the way you want it. It's possible to type directly into a page-layout program but hardly anybody works this way. It's much easier to type into a word processor and save each story or piece of text as a separate file, and this is also the only sensible way of working when there are several contributors to a project. Before we take a detailed look at the main contenders in the field of page layout, here's an introduction to some of the other software you might need in addition to a page-layout program and a word processor.

Bitmap image software

In the early days of desktop publishing, page-layout programs had only the most rudimentary tools for manipulating bitmap images such as photographs, and practically no facilities for creating original graphics other than lines and boxes. Today's page-layout programs offer reasonably sophisticated image-manipulation tools for improving the quality of imported pictures, and built-in drawing tools capable of producing symbols, shapes and 3D text effects as well as web objects such as buttons, hotspots and rollovers.

Despite these enhancements, any professional DTP designer or enthusiastic amateur will prefer to use a separate image editor, not only for simple tasks such as removing flash red eye and colour casts from photographs, but also for applying special effects. Adobe Photoshop is the market-leading image editor but there are plenty of equally capable and much cheaper alternatives such as Adobe Elements and Corel Paint Shop Pro.

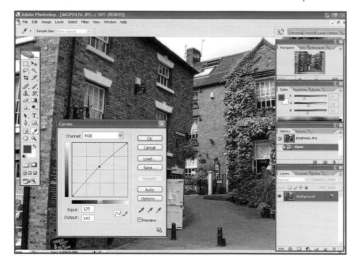

Photoshop offers unprecedented control over image quality plus tight integration with Adobe's desktop-publishing programs, but it is an expensive purchase and mastering its intricacies takes a considerable amount of effort.

Drawing software

For artwork other than photographs and painstakingly-created bitmap illustrations, there are plenty of drawing programs to choose from. These produce so-called vector graphics, which can be scaled to any size without loss of quality. At one end of the scale are easy-to-use drag-and-drop graphics programs such as SmartDraw and Microsoft Visio, which are great for diagrams, business charts and maps. At the other end are sophisticated creative tools such as CorelDRAW and Adobe Illustrator. The high-end programs produce stunning results but take a lot of time to learn, and even though their vendors don't like to admit it, unless you possess some native artistic ability you're unlikely to produce great results with a creative drawing program.

Utility programs

Most regular computer users will already possess most of the utility programs they need. Top of the list is a file-compression program such as WinZip or WinRAR for the PC, or StuffIt for the Mac. These will assist you in decoding compressed files sent in by contributors or images downloaded from the web. Those lucky enough to be running Windows XP can use its built-in compressed folder facility instead.

Another essential for serious DTP work is a scanning program. Most scanners come with a driver that works co-operatively with any image-editing program: you just choose Acquire or Import in your graphics program and the driver kicks into action.

You'll also need a program that can read PDF files but most people already have Acrobat Reader. It's free and can be downloaded from **www.adobe.com**. If you intend to distribute your desktop-published work in PDF files, you'll also need a program that can create PDF files. Some page-layout programs have this facility built into them, but if yours doesn't you can avoid the high cost of buying a full version of Adobe Acrobat by installing a PDF printer driver. You simply go through the motions of printing a document but choose the PDF printer driver instead of your normal printer. Some commercial print houses that prefer to receive work in PDF files will supply their customers with a suitable driver. If you're looking for a third-party PDF printer driver, consider the products available at **www.pdf995.com**. They're completely free to download but the documents they create contain a sponsor's page unless you pay a few dollars to buy a registration key that suppresses the intrusive advertising.

TECHIE CORNER

If you'll be doing a lot of scanning you need a program that gives you greater control over the scanning process, and in particular over colour fidelity, than the standard driver. The solution is a dedicated scanning tool such as VueScan or SilverFast. Of the two, try VueScan first: it's available for both Mac and PC and trial versions can be downloaded free of charge from **www.hamrick.com**. SilverFast can be downloaded from **www.silverfast.com** in several versions, some of which are also available as free trials. Registration costs US$49+VAT for the basic SilverFast SE and up to several hundred dollars for the professional-level products.

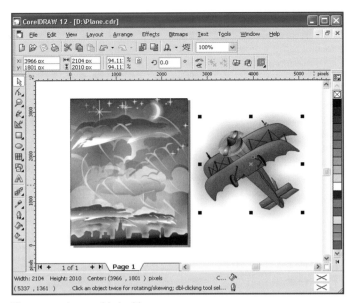

These samples provided with CorelDRAW 12 show what the program can do in the hands of a skilled user.

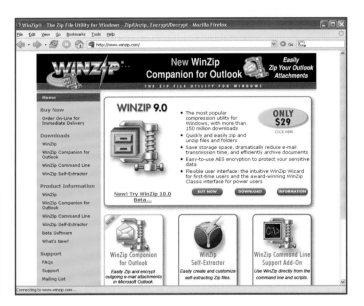

WinZip can be downloaded from **www.winzip.com** as a paid-for program or as a 45-day trial version. For a completely free alternative, try 7-Zip from **www.7-zip.org**.

Popular page-layout programs

Desktop publishing is a specialised area so there are relatively few programs to choose from, but this doesn't mean they're all alike in terms of price or features. In fact, the most expensive program (QuarkXpress 6) costs around ten times as much as the cheapest, yet QuarkXpress is harder to use and arguably less powerful. Despite this it is far and away the leading page-layout software in terms of the number of publishing professionals using it on a daily basis.

In the following reviews, we take a look at seven of the most popular desktop publishing titles. They are listed in order of price, with the most expensive first. QuarkXpress 6, Adobe FrameMaker 7 and Adobe InDesign CS2 are all professional programs with a dedicated following and so, to a lesser extent is Adobe's mid-price program, PageMaker 7. Serif PagePlus 11, Microsoft Publisher 2003 and Apple Pages 2 are all much more affordable and any of them would be a sensible choice for the casual user. The strength of PagePlus is that it offers all the features of its professional rivals at a lower cost, whereas Microsoft Publisher spurns professional features that the home or business user is unlikely to need and instead places emphasis on ease of use and tight integration with the rest of the Microsoft Office products. Apple's Pages 2 is the best solution for Mac users in search of a more casual approach to desktop publishing than the one taken by Adobe's products.

QuarkXpress 6

- Available for Windows and Mac
- Requires Windows 2000, Windows XP or Mac OS X v.10.3 or later
- Minimum hardware requirements for Windows: 128MB RAM, 190MB hard disk space (for installation only), CD-ROM drive

QuarkXpress took over from PageMaker as the professional's preferred page-layout program in the early 1990s. Although it is now outsold by Adobe InDesign, the massive existing user base means that 80 per cent of professional designers still use it. Most commercial printers will accept work in the form of QuarkXpress files, saving you the trouble of converting your publications to PostScript or PDF files (though QuarkXpress is capable of producing both).

The latest version of QuarkXpress boasts unprecedented image-editing controls, enabling you to apply Photoshop-style effects without using Photoshop itself and without making changes to the original image stored on disk. If you intend to work co-operatively with other designers, and particularly if you will be working on a Mac, this is the program to go for, but it's frighteningly expensive.

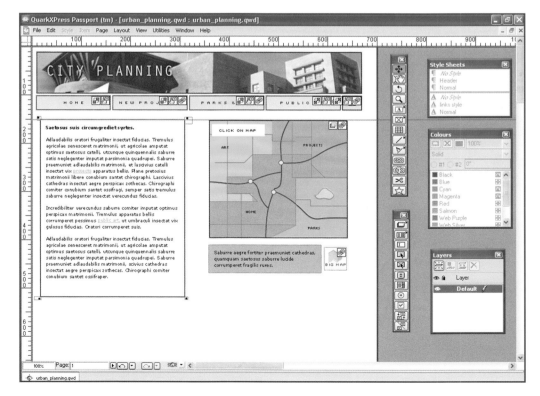

QuarkXpress relies heavily on control palettes (seen here on the right of the screen) but experienced users quickly learn keyboard shortcuts for almost every action.

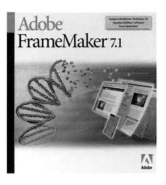

Adobe FrameMaker 7

● Available for Windows and Unix
● Requires Windows 2000, Windows XP or Unix/Solaris 8 or higher
● Minimum hardware requirements for Windows: Pentium III or 4 processor (or equivalent), 256MB RAM, 380MB hard disk space (for installation only), CD-ROM drive

FrameMaker's strength is its collaborative features and its ability to cope with large and complex documents. FrameMaker is not the best choice of layout program for short office documents, posters and flyers, but if you're producing a technical manual for commercial aircraft or an illustrated catalogue of 5000 items, it's ideal. Documents from hundreds of contributors can be compiled with a high level of automation using FrameMaker's structured content organiser, which includes elements of database and graphics management, as well as the ability to insert conditional text according to pre-defined criteria. It bristles with tools for managing enterprise-wide projects and is particularly focussed on producing XML documents.

FrameMaker's design view of a catalogue page is here shown superimposed on its structure view. With the correct structure, you can assemble compound documents that draw their data from a number of sources almost wholly automatically.

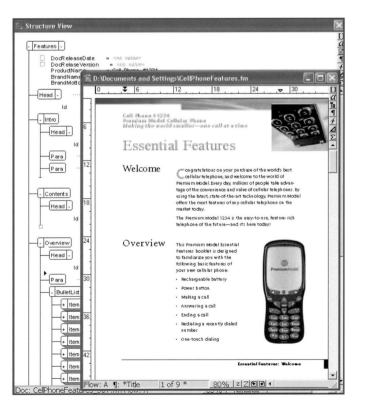

Adobe InDesign CS2

- Available for Windows and Mac
- Requires Windows 2000, Windows XP or Mac OS X v.10.2.8 or later
- Minimum hardware requirements for Windows: Pentium III or 4 processor (or equivalent), 256MB RAM, 850MB hard disk space (for installation only), CD-ROM drive, minimum 1024 x 768 screen resolution

InDesign is Adobe's flagship all-rounder for any type of DTP work. It is sold as a stand-alone program but most users choose to acquire it as part of the Adobe Creative Suite, which is a unified desktop-publishing system that includes Adobe Illustrator and Adobe Photoshop as well as InDesign. Buying all three programs in this way costs less than half as much as buying them separately. InDesign can import styled documents from Microsoft Word and map the Word styles to InDesign styles.

Not surprisingly, given that Adobe invented the PDF, InDesign has superbly flexible PDF file output options, and it can be used to create massive documents up to 18ft x 18ft. It is also exceptionally good for multilingual publications through its understanding of OpenType fonts, through which it is able to set non-Roman style languages such as Cyrillic and Greek. In this respect, it outperforms QuarkXpress 6.

The InDesign interface was designed from the ground up to appeal to both traditional and new users of both Windows and Mac computers. The retractable tool trays on the right of the screen are unobtrusive yet always to hand.

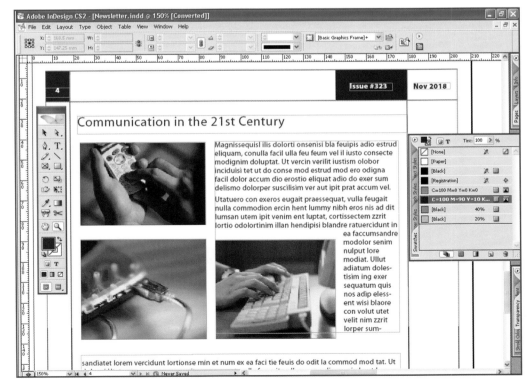

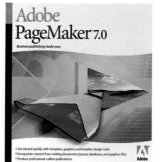

Adobe PageMaker 7
- Available for Windows and Mac
- Requires Windows NT, Windows 2000, Windows XP or Mac OS 9.1 or higher
- Minimum hardware requirements for Windows: Pentium processor (or equivalent), 175MB RAM, 175MB hard disk space (for installation only), CD-ROM drive, minimum 800 x 600 screen resolution

Adobe's mid-priced offering is technically outclassed by the more recent InDesign, but PageMaker has the advantage that it IS PageMaker, the original page-layout program, and it still has a loyal user base of fans who simply don't want to learn anything else. Since Adobe acquired PageMaker from Aldus, the program has undergone several revamps and it still performs as well as ever, especially on older and less powerful equipment. It has also been made easier to use, with the addition of new toolbars and the inclusion of 300 professionally designed templates. You can pick one of these whenever you create a new document, then modify it to suit your purpose. By providing these templates, Adobe is signalling that PageMaker is now aimed at business users rather than design specialists, but the need to maintain compatibility with older versions of the program makes PageMaker less friendly to casual users than it could be.

PageMaker's interface is beginning to look dated, but this is a consequence of the program's ability to run on older PCs with low-resolution graphics and small monitors.

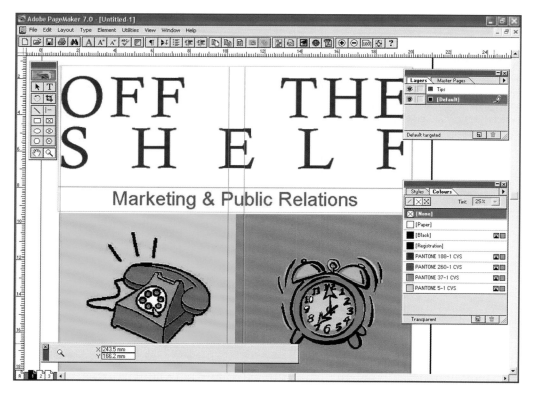

Serif PagePlus 11

- Available for Windows only
- Requires Windows 98SE, Windows Me, Windows 2000 or Windows XP
- Minimum hardware requirements for Windows: Pentium processor (or equivalent), 64MB RAM, 240MB hard disk space (for installation only), CD-ROM drive, minimum 800 x 600 screen resolution

PagePlus was introduced in 1990 as a low-cost alternative to PageMaker for users of Windows PCs. Since then it has been continually developed and its range of features expanded. The current version is slicker than its predecessors, with a new interface and the ability to both load and save PDF files, which is unusual in such a low-cost program. PagePlus successfully straddles the gap between Microsoft Publisher and PageMaker, offering some of the consumer-friendly features of the former and many advanced features from the latter, as well as a few tricks of its own.

PagePlus, like PageMaker, can handle multiple layers that enable you to build modular publications by adding or removing visual elements. It's also possible to link a series of smaller publications into a book-length publication with consistent page-numbering and use of styles throughout. For technical publications and catalogues, database information can be imported from Excel and Access. A number of publication templates are provided, with more available on a free supplementary CD, but casual users will find it less easy to adapt these for their own purposes than those in Microsoft Publisher. PagePlus will appeal to would-be professionals wanting to work in Windows but unwilling to pay the big bucks demanded by Adobe and Quark.

The default appearance of PagePlus is extremely cluttered by a plethora of toolbars plus the Studio tabs on the right of the screen. Fortunately all of these features can be fully customised so it's easy to combine tools and switch them off and on to create more workspace.

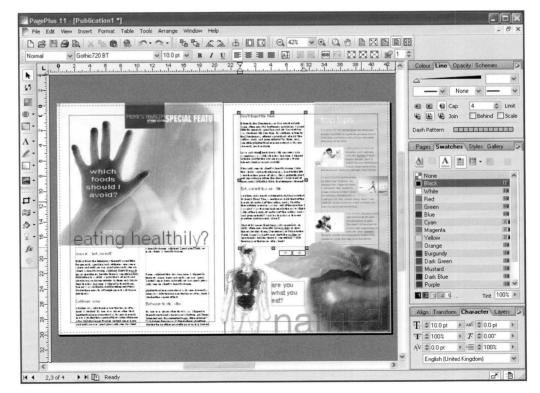

Microsoft Publisher 2003

- Available for Windows only
- Requires Windows 2000 or Windows XP
- Minimum hardware requirements for Windows: Pentium III or 4 processor (or equivalent), 128MB RAM, 250MB hard disk space (for installation only), CD-ROM drive, minimum 800 x 600 screen resolution

Publisher 2003 is part of the Microsoft Office family of products and, like its stablemates, it can be purchased separately or as part of an Office bundle. The emphasis is on ease of use and rapid results, and it seems that Microsoft has devised the program to suit users who only need a page-layout program occasionally, and aren't willing to go through a re-learning process every time they need to use one. Publications can be created from scratch or by using templates. If a template is used, the results can then be customised further using a number of automated formatting tools including design, colour and font schemes that can be imposed on an entire publication with a single mouse click. Enhanced templates, called design sets, are also available: these produce sets of related documents, so that for any sort of special event you can create a website, a brochure, a flyer, a postcard and an invitation all with the same look and theme. Other design sets include personal stationery and specialist business documents.

Wizards are provided to help prepare publications for submission to a commercial printer, and there's also a simple facility that turns any document into a web page and publishes it to a specified web destination. The mail merge and catalog merge facilities combine text and pictures with records from SQL and other database systems, or from any Microsoft Office product. Simple merges can even be made from Microsoft Works. The main weakness of Publisher 2003 is its inability to load or create PDF files.

Publisher 2003 has the standard look and feel of Microsoft Office, with one quirk which is that the Help pane appears on the left of the screen instead of the right.

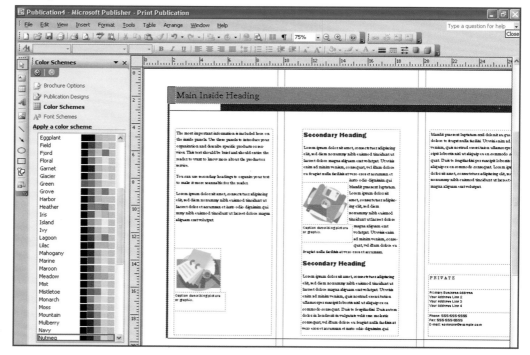

Apple Pages 2

- Available for Mac only
- Minimum requirements are a Macintosh computer with 500MHz Power PC, G4, G5 or Intel Core Duo processor, Mac OS X 10.3.9 or later, 3GB hard disk space, 32MB video memory, 256MB RAM (512MB recommended)

Pages 2 is half of the Apple software package called iWork, the other half being a presentation manager called Keynote 3. Pages 2 is not so much a desktop-publishing package as a word processor on graphical steroids. It can read word-processor files from other programs such as AppleWorks and Word for Windows, and it can save its own work in PDF files suitable for commercial printing.

Over 60 publication templates are included and there's an easy-to-use 3D charting tool and a table-making facility with automated calculations. A built-in image editor permits imported photographs to be enhanced using many of the same adjustments as are available in Apple's iPhoto application, and the Pages 2 graphics tools permit you to create drawings from scratch using lines and curves or by modifying a set of existing shapes such as rectangles, stars and polygons. You can even create mail-merged publications that draw their data from Mac OS X standard address book fields.

The Pages 2 application included with Apple iWork is a dream to use on the new generation of wide-screen TFT monitors.

Fonts and font management

A bewildering variety of fonts is available in all sorts of styles, but more important than their appearance is their provenance. There are three major categories of fonts for use on personal computers and in desktop publishing: PostScript Type 1, TrueType and OpenType.

- PostScript Type 1 fonts are part of the PostScript page description language and each font is supplied as a pair of files. One defines the font that is displayed on screen and the other the font that is used by the printer. PostScript Type 1 files are the ones to use on a Macintosh. They are available for Windows, but the Windows versions are not interchangeable with Mac versions and they may necessitate the use of a control program called Adobe Type Manager (provided free with commercially available Type 1 font packages). These are the fonts to use if you are a professional desktop publisher outputting for a commercial printer.

- TrueType fonts do the same job as PostScript Type 1 fonts. A basic set is provided free with Windows, and they can also be used on Mac computers. A type manager is not required for either Mac or PC, and most PostScript printers and image setters can handle TrueType fonts, although not with the same reliability as PostScript Type 1 fonts. These are the fonts to use if you are a casual desktop publisher, especially if you are printing your own work.

- OpenType fonts are an extension of the TrueType family, embodying PostScript-type information. They are true cross-platform fonts, so the same fonts will work on both Mac and PC. Any computer that can use TrueType fonts is also able to use OpenType fonts, but not all programs can make use of the additional features of OpenType fonts, which include a wider range of characters and a more sophisticated set of typographic controls.

Even if you use TrueType or OpenType fonts, which do not require a type manager to be installed, it can still be advantageous to install one. This is because fonts take a considerable time to load and, if a great many are installed, they can impair the performance of the computer. A type manager allows you to control which fonts are always available and which should be ignored unless they are specifically required. In this way you can maintain an extensive bank of fonts without degrading the day-to-day performance of your computer. A reliable and cheap (US$25) font manager for Windows is Printer's Apprentice, downloadable from the distributor at **www.loseyourmind.com**. A more sophisticated set of alternatives is available from **www.extensis.com**. Suitcase Fusion is a good choice for the Mac and Suitcase for Windows is ideal for PCs.

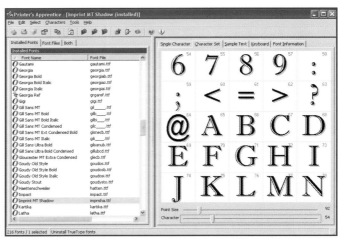

Printer's Apprentice works with PostScript, OpenType and TrueType fonts with equal ease, enabling you to install and disable any font at will.

Windows XP and Mac OS X can handle PostScript Type 1 fonts without a type manager. Users of earlier versions of the Windows and Mac operating systems can download Adobe Type Manager Light, free of charge, from **www.adobe.com/products/atmlight**

Choosing and using a desktop printer

A desktop printer is an essential part of any desktop-publishing system. You'll use it to proof your publications before sending them to a commercial print shop and to produce the printouts that many print shops prefer to receive along with electronic source files. You might even choose to print final copies yourself using a desktop printer, which can be an attractive option where relatively few copies are required. The definition of relatively few in this context depends on whether you own an inkjet printer or a laser printer: for inkjet printers, relatively few means no more than a handful, but for laser printers it might mean several hundreds of copies.

Of the many technologies used by personal computer printers, the two that are most suitable for desktop-publishing tasks are inkjet and laser printers. Other technologies such as dye sublimation, thermal transfer and solid ink have their uses, particularly for high-quality graphical and photographic output, but inkjet and laser printers are the best and most cost-effective all-rounder printers for DTP work.

Canon calls its inkjet printers 'bubble jet' printers. This model i455 is an A4 printer that can also be connected directly to a digital camera via a USB cable, enabling snapshots to be printed without a PC.

Inkjet printers

Inkjet printers are cheap to buy, reasonably fast, and capable of excellent colour output, but for the best results you need expensive coated papers rather than standard photocopier paper. The refills for inkjet printers are also expensive, and it is now common knowledge that the main reason inkjet printers are so cheap is that manufacturers know they will be able to extract the cost of the printer many times over from customers who are tied to their proprietary cartridges for the life of the printer. Sadly, every printer manufacturer uses a unique cartridge design and there is no such thing as a generic printer cartridge that's cheaply available from third-party manufacturers. There are ink-refill systems, of course, but these are messy and inconvenient, and many users consider the results from refilled cartridges to be inferior to genuine inks from the printer manufacturer.

All inkjet printers work by directing streams of different coloured inks through very fine nozzles onto paper. As the paper moves through the printer, the print head moves from side to side across the paper, eventually covering all parts of the page with the exception of a narrow border on all four sides. Most inkjet printers contain four inks (cyan, magenta, yellow and black) and all other colours are created by juxtaposing dots of these four colours with great precision. Using coated papers, many inkjets can lay down 1440 x 1440 coloured dots per square inch, but with cheaper papers a lower resolution has to be used or the dots

will run together as the paper absorbs the ink, resulting in a blurry image and muddy colours.

Numerous special papers are available in a range of colours and textures, including woven surfaces and metallic finishes. Inkjet printers can also accept relatively stiff card stock, as well as specialist materials including thermal transfer paper for iron-on T-shirt designs, and transparent film for use with overhead projectors.

Although the paper-handling capability of a standard inkjet printer is any size up to A4, paper trays tend to hold only 50–100 sheets, making an inkjet printer unsuitable for large print runs unless supplementary paper trays and feeders are available. The other limiting factor is print speed. Manufacturers claim their printers can produce up to 20 pages per minute, but this is only under ideal laboratory conditions using very simple documents. Complex A4 documents with pictures, where most of the page needs to be printed, might take a minute or more per page. It's always better to determine print speeds from independent reviews rather than a manufacturer's optimistic specifications.

Inkjet printers are not limited to three coloured inks plus black: this one from Hewlett Packard takes additional cyan and magenta cartridges to improve the quality of its photographic output.

Laser printers

In recent years, the prices of laser printers have plummeted even more spectacularly than those of inkjet printers, and for much the same reasons: massive economies of scale make them cheaper to produce and the anticipation of ongoing profits from the sales of toner and consumables encourages manufacturers to sell laser printers at close to cost price.

While monochrome inkjet printers are very rare, monochrome laser printers are still readily available, with entry-level models costing under £100. The entry point for colour lasers is around £200 with the more robust and versatile models checking in at around twice the price.

Even if you've never used a laser printer, the technology will be familiar because of its similarity to photocopying. It involves transferring powdered toner from an electrostatic drum onto a sheet of paper and then using heat to fuse the toner permanently into the paper to produce a sharp, dry, permanent image. There's something of a wait (up to a minute) for the first page to be processed, but subsequent pages arrive at the printer's rated speed, which for a budget printer will be around 20 pages per minute monochrome or 5 pages per minute in full colour. The

This entry-level monochrome personal laser from Canon is small enough to sit next to a PC but has only a 125-sheet paper capacity.

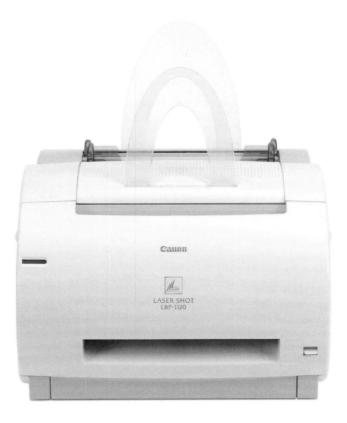

reason for the discrepancy is that most printers use four passes to produce a colour image: one for each of the four toner colours.

Colour toners are replaced individually, so there's no waste, but a complete replacement pack (cyan, magenta, yellow and black) is likely to cost around £250, which in some cases is more than the printer itself. New printers tend to come equipped with partially-filled toner packs, good for fewer than 1500 pages, but full-price replacements are generally capable of 4000 pages or more. Colour and monochrome laser printers have other components that need replacing at different intervals. The electrostatic drum and the fuser unit are the most expensive of these, but the former will last for several changes of toner and the fuser unit is generally good for at least 100,000 copies. Nevertheless, the true cost of ownership of a laser printer bears no relation to its purchase price, and any potential purchaser would do well to compare the replacement costs and intervals of all its consumables before selecting a suitable model.

Another detail to check is the printer's duty cycle. This tells you how many pages it can be expected to handle per month, which is significant if you're going to use the printer to produce bulk

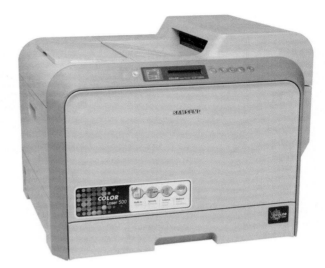

Samsung's CLP-510 colour laser printer is one of the cheapest to feature a built-in duplex paper handler that can print on both sides of the paper. On most entry-level printers, duplex printing is either unavailable or an expensive extra.

A complete set of toners for a colour laser printer can cost more than the printer itself.

copies rather than just proofs. Duty cycles range from 15,000 to 200,000 pages per month.

A laser printer is, in effect, a computer in its own right, with its own processor and its own memory (see the next section). The minimum memory for DTP work is 32MB, but 64MB is preferable. Most printers can have their memory upgraded with plug-in RAM cards. Older and very basic laser printers offer a maximum resolution of 300 x 300dpi but most are capable of 600 x 600dpi, which is good enough for general DTP work. For high-quality output, printers with a resolution of 1200 x 1200dpi are readily available but beyond this you move into commercial printing territory and prices.

You should beware of spurious claims for resolution: a manufacturer claiming 600 x 2400dpi is almost certainly using some form of software manipulation to boost the apparent quality. For example, Hewlett Packard claims 2400 x 2400dpi for its Color LaserJet 3500, but only when the company's proprietary resolution-enhancement technology is employed; the true resolution is actually 600 x 600dpi. To be fair, HP makes this clear in the specifications by listing 600dpi as the 'engine resolution'; other manufacturers are sometimes less forthcoming.

Laser printer languages

When you buy a printer it comes with a printer driver for your computer, and it is through this that you control most of the

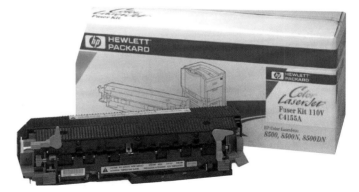

Fuser units need to be replaced periodically. This one from Hewlett Packard simply slots in, but some printers require an expensive visit from a service mechanic. It's worth checking before you buy to see how many internal components require regular replacement (it could be as many as nine) and whether they are user-upgradeable.

If you're not sure whether laser-printed output will be suitable for your desktop-published material, visit **www.konicaminoltaprinters. co.uk** and choose a printer. You may then upload a sample of your work and receive a free printout of your work produced on any of the company's machines.

printer's functions. Naturally you can reasonably expect the driver to be capable of transferring onto paper whatever you create on screen with your desktop-publishing software, but it's worth digging a little deeper into how the printer generates its pages. Laser printers either rely on Windows to do all the work for them, or they use a page description language to generate their output.

The two most common page description languages are PCL and PostScript, though there are others which are proprietary to specific printer manufacturers. If your printer uses a page description language, it doesn't really matter which one if you are going to do your own printing, but you should be aware that all commercial printing devices use PostScript, so if your printer can use it too, you are guaranteed that the proofs you produce on your desktop will be exactly the same as the final commercially printed output. This will usually be the case even if your printer uses PCL, but anyone contemplating taking on professional DTP work should definitely opt for a PostScript printer, simply to eliminate any doubt. PostScript printers are generally dearer than their non-PostScript equivalents.

If Windows is expected to do the work, as it is in most budget laser printers, the printer will be described in one of three ways: as host-based, GDI or WPS. These are really just different ways of saying the same thing. The significance is that a host-based printer does not contain its own processor, fonts or memory: it relies on the PC to do the processing instead. The main disadvantage of this is that if your PC is already straining under the load, a host-based printer will simply aggravate the problem, but in terms of output quality a host-based printer is as good as one with a built-in page description language. If your PC has a fast processor and plenty of memory, there's no reason not to choose a host-based device.

The bottom line – inkjet or laser?

If you intend to do your own printing instead of sending it away, you definitely need a laser printer. An inkjet printer can't cope with very high volumes of work, and in any case the true cost per page of inkjet printing (ignoring manufacturers' claims) is generally reckoned to be two or three times higher than laser printing. Other advantages of laser printers are:

- Fast printing, especially in monochrome
- Permanent copies that will not smudge or smear
- Less attention required during printing
- Larger paper trays that permit longer unattended print runs
- No colour blur caused by ink absorption when using cheap paper
- Automatic double-sided printing if the printer is a duplex model

If your printer will only be used for proofing, the decision to buy laser or inkjet will depend on what else you use it for. The main strengths of an inkjet printer are:

- Photographic-quality output on glossy paper
- The ability to accept a range of specialist printing materials and papers in varying weights

The latest mid-priced laser printers can produce glossy photographic output on special paper, but the results are not quite as impressive as inkjet images, and the initial outlay for a suitable laser printer will be considerably higher. This makes an inkjet printer a better choice if you wish to print a small number of documents and pictures at high quality, and especially if you wish to use special papers or printing media. Inkjet printing is also the way to go if you want to print documents larger than A4. An A3 colour inkjet printer cost hundreds of pounds, instead of the thousands you'd be required to stump up for an A3 colour laser.

In nearly all other cases, a laser printer is the better choice for DTP work because it produces durable, smudge-free printouts faster and more cheaply than an inkjet printer. And don't think you have to have colour: a monochrome laser printer is fine for proofing any kind of publication, but its lack of colour limits its usefulness as a final output device.

Glossy paper for laser printers doesn't make prints appear sharper in the same way that it does with inkjet printers, but it does look and feel very professional. Photos printed on ordinary paper are perfectly acceptable for newsletter-style publications, so you can save the expensive glossy stuff for covers and inserts.

For presentation work and posters, this Epson Stylus Pro 4000 printer is ideal. It uses eight separate ink cartridges and accepts papers up to A2 in size. However its price, size and running costs make it unsuitable for day-to-day print jobs.

If you don't need fax facilities you can take home a printer/copier/scanner like this one for less than £100. It also prints directly from digital camera memory cards.

Multifunction devices

A multifunction device, sometimes called a 'mopier', combines the features of a printer, a scanner, a fax machine and a copier in a single unit. The price is usually equal to the cost of a printer and scanner, with the fax and copier capabilities thrown in. Bear in mind that with a separate printer and scanner you can emulate a copier anyway, so what you really get is a free fax machine.

Multifunction printers contain colour inkjet or monochrome laser print engines, and the same comments made earlier about these can also be applied to multifunction devices. The main advantage of a combined device is that it saves space. You might also find it useful that only one connection is required to the PC and to the mains supply. The disadvantages are relatively minor. The main one is that if a single component within the device breaks down or wears out, you have to replace everything. Other considerations are that it is not possible to print and scan at the same time, and the scanning performance may not be equal to that of a separate flatbed scanner.

Generally speaking, a multifunction printer is a great asset in a small office where space is limited and where it will be called upon to perform general duties, but for desktop publishing purposes, and especially for anybody considering doing their own bulk printing, it's an inferior option to a stand-alone printer.

PART 1

Setting up your hardware in Windows

It doesn't matter how carefully you select your hardware and how much you pay for it; if the individual components are not set up properly they won't deliver their best performance. The key components in desktop publishing are monitors, printers and scanners. Not only do these have to be set up with the correct drivers and settings for Windows, they also have to be calibrated or profiled so that the colours generated by the scanner and the colours you see on the monitor match the colours output by your printer. Colour consistency between devices is even more important if your publications are to be sent to a commercial printer, because wherever possible you will also try to match the colours from your system with the colours produced by the remote printer.

We'll take each device in turn, starting with the monitor, and examine how it should best be configured, and then we'll look at some general considerations regarding colour matching. Because this book is aimed at non-professional users who don't have access to expensive test equipment and software, for the most part we'll look at solutions that can be implemented with free software or by using simple manual procedures.

Setting up a monitor

The monitor is your window into the PC's world and there are very few things you can do with your computer that don't involve looking at it. Desktop publishing requires constant use of the monitor so it's important that the picture is as bright, sharp, flicker-free and clear as possible, and that the monitor displays colours which are true to life.

You shouldn't start adjusting the monitor until the rest of the graphics system is correctly configured. Regardless of whether graphics are generated by a separate card or an integrated controller on the computer's motherboard, your first task is to make sure that the most up-to-date driver for the display adapter is installed. It is through this driver that the display adapter talks to Windows, and hence to the monitor; because drivers are constantly being improved, you cannot assume that the one supplied with your computer is the most recent or the best.

To check which display adapter and driver are currently in use, right-click on a blank area of the Windows desktop and select Properties. When the Display Properties dialogue box opens, click the Settings tab. Just below the picture of a monitor you'll see a message describing the monitor and display adapter: it will say something such as 'NEC Multisync M600 on ATI Radeon X800' or 'CM1977FS on NVIDIA GeForce 4'. The first part of the description is the monitor and the second is the display adapter.

Below the message, you'll see slider controls for adjusting the resolution of the monitor and the colour quality, which between them determine how much information you can fit on the screen and how many colours will be viewable. The best resolution for you depends on how big your monitor is and how sharp your eyes are, but for desktop-publishing work consider 1024 x 768 pixels as a minimum, and whatever your monitor can display sharply and your eyes can see without strain as the maximum. The best colour setting is 32 bit. 16 bit is too low for desktop publishing with pictures, and 24 bit, if it is offered, is a compromise. If you're not offered 32 bit as an option, you either have a very old computer or an antiquated display adapter, and it might be time to consider updating one or the other. But before you dash out to the nearest computer superstore and part with hard-earned cash, read on to see if all you need is a new driver.

If the monitor is described as a generic VGA or Plug and Play model this means you are using standard Windows drivers and you could get better performance from your monitor by installing the drivers from the CD or floppy disk supplied with it, but first make sure you have the best driver installed for your display adapter. To do this, click the Advanced button in the Display Properties dialogue box, and then click on the Adapter tab. Now click the Properties button and a separate dialogue box for display adapter properties will be displayed. Click the Driver tab in this secondary dialogue box and you will be able to read off both the date of the driver and its version number.

Time now to log onto the internet and search the web for more up-to-date drivers. Your first stop is the website of your computer's manufacturer or, failing this, the supplier of its display adapter. Once you're there, click the Support option and find the Download section. Look for a driver that has a higher version number or later date than the one you already have. Make sure you specify which version of Windows you're using because XP drivers are often different to those for earlier versions. If there is a more recent driver, download and install it according to the manufacturer's instructions, or use the Update Driver button in the Display Properties dialogue box. Only when you've done this, or at least assured yourself that you're already using the latest driver, are you ready to set up the monitor itself.

You're probably already familiar with your monitor's built-in controls for brightness and contrast, and you might also have used some of the geometrical controls that influence the width and height of the screen and ensure that circles look circular and straight lines look straight. What you can't do with the built-in monitor controls is adjust the display gamma. Gamma is an adjustment affecting the appearance of mid-range colours but, unlike brightness and contrast, the setting of gamma has no impact on black or white levels, which makes it a very important tool for colour correction. A consortium of image-device manufacturers together with Microsoft came up with a standard way of defining colour on any device called sRGB.

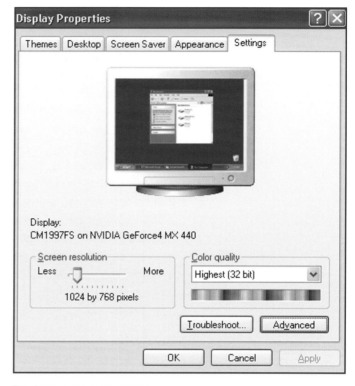

The Settings tab in the Display Properties dialogue box is where you can determine which graphics controller and monitor are in use, and where you can make basic changes to picture quality.

Part of this standard is a gamma level of 2.2, and it is only by setting your monitor to this level that you can expect the colours you print to match the colours you see on screen.

With Adobe Photoshop and Adobe Elements comes a neat little utility called Adobe Gamma, which does two things: it permits the adjustment of monitor gamma using a simple step-by-step visual technique, and it comes with a loader module that automatically applies your chosen settings every time you start Windows or your Mac. If you don't have a copy of Adobe Gamma you can download a free program that does all the same things and more from **www.praxisoft.com**. It's called WiziWYG and it comes in different flavours for Windows XP and for earlier versions of Windows. Make sure you download and install the correct version, then read the following quick guide to using it.

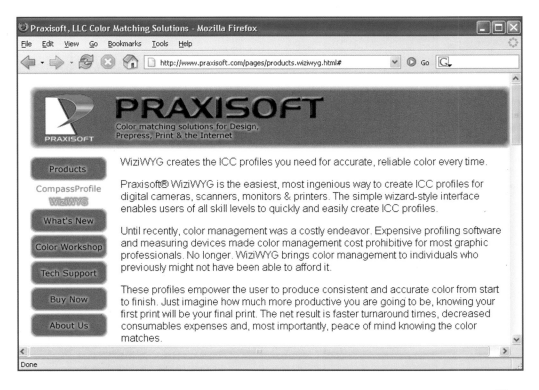

There's no point downloading drivers for your display adapter unless you know the correct type of adapter and the version number of the current drivers. This information is available in the Display Properties dialogue boxes.

Praxisoft distributes WiziWYG free of charge as a means of drawing attention to the company's professional range of calibration and colour management products.

Make sure that your monitor has reached its normal operating temperature (15–30 minutes) and adjust the room lighting so that it is adequately but not too brightly lit. In particular, make sure there are no reflections on the screen from nearby windows. The next thing to do is set the colour temperature of your monitor to 6500K, as laid down in the sRGB standard you are aiming to comply with. The setting of the colour temperature is done from within your monitor's on-screen control panel, which will look something like this example. You'll probably find the colour temperature is initially set to 9300K, which is very bright and with a faint blue cast. Don't worry if the screen looks rather dull after making the change to 6500K. You'll put this right in the following steps.

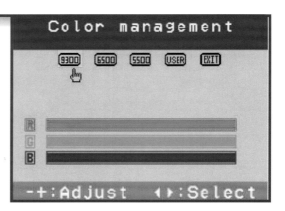

Start WiziWYG and wait a few seconds for the splash screen to disappear. On the opening screen you'll see that WiziWYG can be used to profile scanners, printers and monitors, but scanners and printers can only be calibrated with the help of additional test equipment. You should therefore ignore these options, click on the monitor icon to select it, and then click Next.

On the next screen, WiziWYG will realise you do not have a hardware colorimeter attached to your PC and will preselect the Visual No Colorimeter option for you. Just click Next to proceed to the screen shown here. Using the controls on your monitor, set the contrast and brightness to 100 per cent, then decrease the brightness until you can barely see the smaller, paler squares inside the black squares. Now decrease the contrast until the inner squares within the white squares have almost disappeared. Click Next.

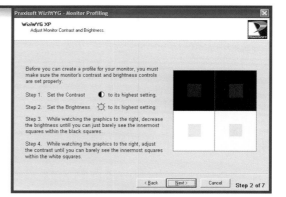

If you found it difficult to adjust the inner squares in Step 3 or you couldn't see them at all, there's an alternative way of setting brightness and contrast by pointing your web browser to the monitor test patterns at **http://brighamrad.harvard.edu/research/topics/vispercep/tutorial.html**. You'll find full instructions there on using the chart, but basically all you need do is adjust the brightness and contrast until you can differentiate all the grey boxes from black to white. When you've done this, use Alt+Tab to switch back to WiziWYG.

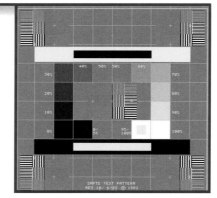

5

On this screen, you adjust overall tonal balance by making adjustments to each colour individually. Use the slider controls or the up/down arrows to make the inner square of each colour match the outer square. This is easier if you can position yourself 2–3 metres from your monitor but, if your mouse cable won't permit this, most people find they can achieve the same effect by squinting. Just don't do this when there are other people around or they'll think you've been drinking. When you've finished, click Next.

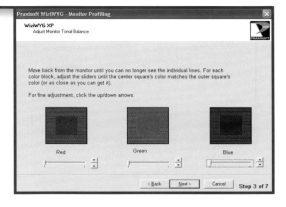

6

On the next screen, select your monitor type by manufacturer. If your manufacturer isn't there, select Generic sRGB monitor instead, then click Next to proceed to the screen shown here. You must now select the D65 White Point, which is the closest match to the 6500K colour temperature you set earlier, and then select a gamma setting of 2.20 Std PC or TV. Some monitors, including Trinitron, have multiple White Points. If yours is one of these, you'll see an intermediate screen asking you to choose which one to use. Select the D65 option.

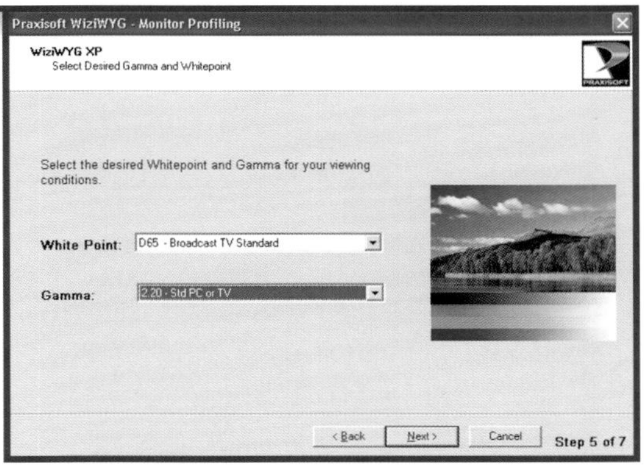

7

On this screen you save the settings as a profile that can be used as part of an advanced colour management scheme. Whether you ever use this profile explicitly is irrelevant. What really matters is that in saving the profile you also configure WiziWYG to load the settings you've just defined every time Windows starts up. Click the button labelled Name the Monitor Profile, and when a Save As dialogue box appears, call the profile 'WiziWYG monitor'. Click Save. To complete the process you must now click the Create Profile button, and then click Finish.

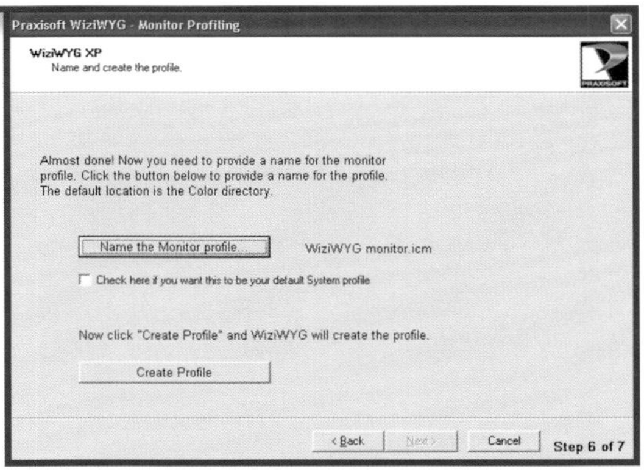

8

That's all there is to it: your WiziWYG configuration will be applied every time you start Windows. If you prefer the old pre-WiziWYG screen settings, which might be the case if you play games or watch movies on your PC, you can prevent the revised ones being applied by removing the WiziWYG entry from the Startup section of the Windows Start menu. Simply drag it to the Windows desktop and leave it there. From then on, when you start Windows you'll have your old settings back, but when you want colour fidelity for DTP or graphics work you can double-click the WiziWYG shortcut on the desktop.

Setting up a printer

1

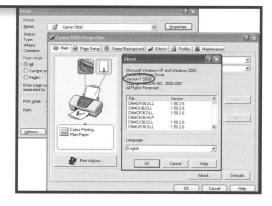

Every printer comes with an installation CD and instructions for connecting the printer to a PC and installing its driver. Assuming you've done all this and the printer is working normally within Windows, the next step is to check that the driver supplied by the manufacturer is the most up-to-date one. One way of doing this is to use the Print command in any application and, when the Print dialogue box appears, click Properties. This will invoke the Properties dialogue box for your specific printer, and you can then use its About button to read details of the driver.

2

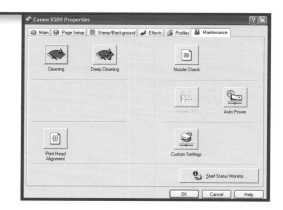

Armed with this information, visit the website of your printer manufacturer and in the Support or Download section, check to see if there is a driver with a later version than yours. If there is, download and install it. The driver should come with detailed installation instructions. If not, the usual procedure is to double-click the file you've downloaded to expand its contents into a folder. Remove the existing printer driver using the Add/Remove Programs feature in the Windows Control Panel. Turn off your printer's power and then double-click on Setup.exe to start installing the new driver. The installation program will prompt you to turn on the printer at the appropriate time.

3

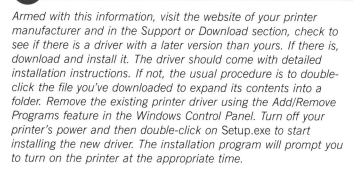

Before conducting any tests to see if the output from your printer matches the display on the monitor, it's important to follow any set-up procedures recommended by the printer's manufacturer. These might involve printing a test page or starting a cleaning cycle, and in the case of inkjet printers cleaning the nozzles and aligning the print head. All of these options should be accessible in the Maintenance section of the printer's Properties dialogue box, which can be invoked as described in Step 1.

4

*You'll need a test file to print. It should include a wide range of colours, as many shades of grey as possible, and preferably some flesh tones and shadows. If you don't have a suitable file, try a web search for 'printer test image' and download one that takes your fancy. This one was found at **www.robyncolor.com**. Load the test file into your favourite graphics program, and then print it on the paper you normally use, using the fit-to-page option and whatever quality setting is recommended for the paper you've chosen. There's no point in calibrating your printer to produce superb colours on expensive glossy media if you'll be doing most of your printing on ordinary matt white paper.*

5

Allow the print to dry, and then compare it with the test image on the monitor screen. You will never get a perfect match between the RGB image on a monitor and the inks or toners used by a printer but the skin tones should look natural, solid colours should be equally saturated and greys should have equal intensity and bear no traces of any colour casts. In many cases, with a correctly adjusted monitor, the output from the printer should be a pretty close match with the screen and the printer may not need further adjustment at all but, if it does, you can apply the necessary corrections within the printer driver. This table indicates which colours may need to be increased or decreased in order to correct each type of colour inconsistency.

Colour cast	Increase these colours	Or decrease these colours
Red	C	Y, M
Yellow	C, M	Y
Green	M	C, Y
Cyan	Y, M	C
Blue	Y	C, M
Magenta	C, Y	M

6

Every printer driver is different in terms of where the colour adjustment controls can be found, but they are usually on the main screen of the driver or in a Printing Preferences section. In this Canon printer driver, there is a Colour Adjustment option on the main screen, which by default is set to Auto. If you change this to Manual, the Set button becomes active and you can click it to proceed to a secondary window where the changes can be implemented.

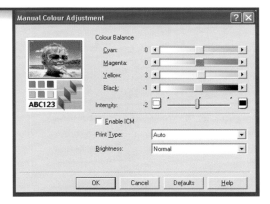

7

Colour adjustment screens are usually equipped with spinners or slider controls like those shown here. Don't make too many adjustments at one time. Start by adjusting the intensity if all the colours look weak, and then make another test print. Next, correct any colour casts and make another test print, and possibly several more if you don't get it right first time. Finally, use the black control to fix any discrepancies in grey levels and make yet more test prints. Note down on paper the changes you have made.

8

In some printer drivers there is the option to save a set of colour adjustments and assign a name to them for future use, but in the sample Canon printer driver shown here the settings are for the current session only. To use the same settings for future print runs, it is necessary to apply the colour changes via the Windows Control Panel instead of while printing an actual document. In this way, they become the default settings for every print job. Simply find your printer in the Control Panel, right-click and select Properties, apply the adjustments you've noted down, and then click OK.

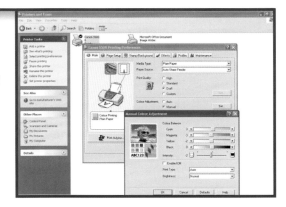

Setting up a scanner

In many respects setting up a scanner is similar to setting up a printer. As with a printer, it's important to have the most up-to-date driver installed so you should check this first. Very little additional configuration is necessary apart from basic calibration, which the scanner performs for itself when it is first switched on or whenever its driver is updated. You may be asked to insert a

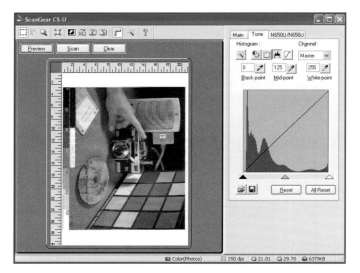

There are facilities within scanner drivers to correct colour discrepancies on a preview made before the actual scan, but many users prefer to carry out corrections afterwards in a more powerful program.

TECHIE CORNER

It is also possible to calibrate a scanner using more advanced techniques, but you can't do it properly without a professionally-produced colour target such as the IT8, which is available from Kodak or supplied as part of a calibration software package. The target has to be scanned and compared with an electronic version of itself to determine where any colour inconsistencies lie. Having done this, a colour profile can be stored on the hard disk and used as part of a formal colour management scheme (see below).

This is a mock up of an IT8 colour test card. They are quite expensive to buy because each one has to be carefully printed and individually checked to ensure its colours are accurate.

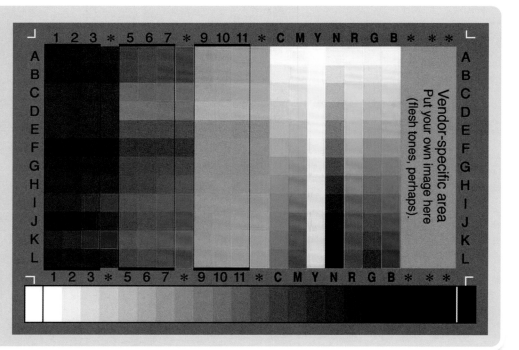

sheet of white paper, after which the scanner will spend a minute or so examining itself. What the scanner does during this time is to adjust its white balance so that colours are rendered faithfully.

For non-professional DTP users, colour management is by no means essential, and if your monitor, printer and scanner have been correctly set up as described, the chances are that the colours of scanned images will be fine. Any corrections to individual scans that may be necessary can be made using an image-editing program after the scan has been saved to disk.

Colour management

Colour management (or color management, as Microsoft calls it) has been built into every version of Windows from 98 onwards. The system used in Windows XP is called ICM 2.0, which stands for Image Colour Management, as developed by the International Colour Consortium.

The way it works is that every device that uses colour – be it a monitor, desktop printer, scanner or commercial output device – is supplied with an ICM profile that can be loaded into Windows. You may never have heard of ICM profiles because they are installed automatically along with device drivers, but Windows knows where they are (in Windows XP, a sub-folder of Windows called system32\spool\drivers\color).

Before you can understand what a profile does, you need to

If you want to satisfy yourself that your hardware devices are using colour management and have ICM profiles installed, look on the Color Management tab of each device's Properties dialogue box.

know a little bit more about why there's a problem getting colours to match across different devices. It's all to do with colour spaces and gamuts. These two unfamiliar terms are not as threatening as they seem.

Every device has a 'colour space' in which it is said to operate. For a monitor, the RGB colour space defines all the available colours by specifying amounts of red, green and blue light. Printers use the CMYK colour space, in which every colour is defined by the percentages of cyan, magenta, yellow and black that make it up.

There are several other colour spaces in general use. The one you're most likely to encounter when using an image-editing program is HSL, which defines colours by their hue, saturation and lightness.

Because of the different ways of defining colours within each colour space, the situation often arises when there is no exact match in CMYK for a colour that exists in RGB. This problem raises its head every time you send publications based on RGB colours to a printer that uses CMYK colours. Although the printer will make a very close approximation to the correct colour, it won't be exactly the same. To make matters worse, every device has a different 'gamut' (the number of colours from its colour space that it can actually print or display). The gamut is smaller than the full range of colours in the colour space because of the limitations of CCD sensors, monitor phosphors, printer ink and the other physical components used to generate colours.

ICM profiles

Bearing these problems in mind, let's return to the topic of ICM profiles and what exactly they are for. Their job is to let Windows know the precise capabilities of each device in terms of the colour space it uses and the gamut of colours available to it. Windows can then translate colours between devices, keeping them as close as possible to the original colours but within the design limitations of each device. Much of this colour matching is handled by Windows in the background and is of no concern to ordinary users, but some programs can hook into the Windows colour management system and put direct control of colour management into the hands of the operator. Most image-editing programs and any desktop-publishing program aimed at professional users will feature user-definable colour management controls. Using these, you can determine exactly which ICM profiles you want the program to use. For example, when designing publications you intend to print yourself, you'll use the ICM profile of your own printer, but when you intend to send work to a commercial printer you can use the ICM profile of the actual device that will do the final printing.

Colour management sounds great in theory, but it's very difficult to implement in practise because the ICM profiles included with computer hardware are not accurate enough. You can't expect every printer of a particular make and model to perform identically to its stable mates, yet they all come with the

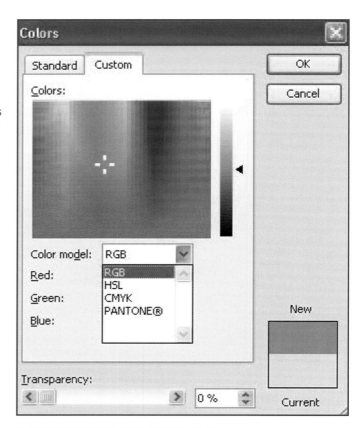

In Microsoft Publisher, there are four colour models (colour spaces) you can use when defining and picking colours. In general, it's always best to stick with RGB unless you have a special purpose in mind. Documents intended for commercial printing can be converted prior to printing using Tools > Commercial Printing Tools > Color Printing > CMYK.

The colour management options in Paint Shop Pro can emulate a printer other than the one attached to the system. The manual advises you not to use colour management unless you are in possession of correctly calibrated customised profiles for every device connected to the system.

same profile. And when you consider the wide range of inks and papers available, the discrepancies between devices are even greater. For colour management to work effectively you need to create a customised profile for every device in your system and, in the case of printers, for every type of paper. These profiles will need to be updated regularly because the profile of any device changes over time as its components are used, and the profiles can only be accurately defined using proper calibration equipment and industry standard test files and test cards.

Tips on working without colour management

If you're setting yourself up as professional desktop publisher doing work for other people, you have to bite the financial bullet (and take the time) to set up and use proper colour management procedures in every aspect of your work. Casual business users and private users really don't need to bother with it: for them it's enough to carefully calibrate monitors and printers as described earlier. However, there's still the problem of ensuring that when you send work to be printed commercially, the printed colours match your own original designs.

One solution is to find a printer willing to calibrate the final output to match your own printouts. All you have to do is provide high-quality proofs from your own printer along with the files to be printed.

Another approach is to ask the printer to supply you with a colour chart printed on the final output device in which each colour has its CMYK values printed. Pantone is probably the best known colour-matching scheme for ink and paper and it is one that every print shop can handle.

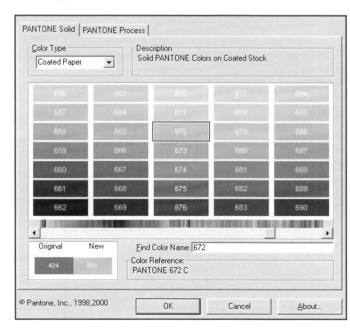

The palettes from which Pantone colours are chosen in Microsoft Publisher. Note that the rendering of Pantone colours on screen is only an approximation: you need a printed colour swatch to see how colours will actually print.

PART 2 **Basic DTP techniques**

PART 2 Design and layout

All the practical examples and step-by-step guides in this book can be completed using Microsoft Publisher 2003, but the techniques demonstrated can be applied within any other desktop-publishing program. If you don't already own Publisher and you're not planning on buying it, you can nevertheless follow the practical examples by ordering a free 30-day evaluation kit for Publisher 2003. It comes on CD, complete with a Getting Started manual and additional resources, and is completely free except for a small shipping charge. The evaluation kit is available worldwide and can be ordered at **www.microsoft.com/office/ publisher/prodinfo/trial.mspx**. There is no difference between the evaluation kit and the full retail version, apart from the time limitation, and if you decide to go on using Publisher 2003 after the end of the trial period you can purchase a permanent activation code from Microsoft.

Once you have installed Publisher be sure to click the Check for Updates option on its Help menu. An essential update if you are to follow the step-by-step guides in this book is Office 2003

Before you order the trial version of Microsoft Publisher 2003 make sure you haven't already got a copy. It's included with the Microsoft Office 2003 Small Business and Professional editions.

The free version of PagePlus comes with just a few sample templates to get you started, but once you've installed the program you can choose from literally hundreds more on the website.

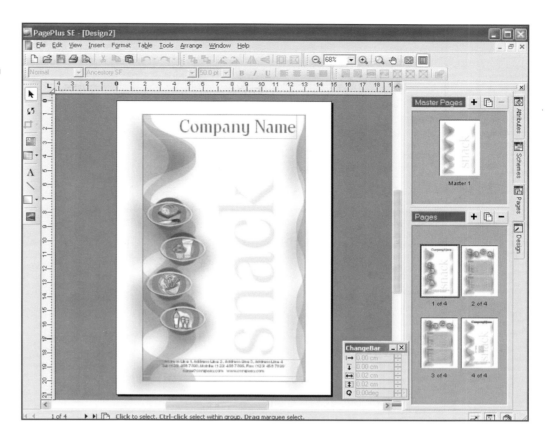

Service Pack 2, which contains not only a number of bug fixes but also some enhancements to Microsoft Publisher.

Readers who already own a desktop-publishing program from another vendor can follow the practical examples using their own software. Shortcut keystrokes and menu commands will sometimes differ, but the principles of desktop publishing are well established so there is no problem simulating the features of Publisher in another program. If you don't already have DTP software, and you can't wait for the Publisher 2003 evaluation kit to arrive through the post, you can download a free copy of PagePlus SE from **www.freeserifsoftware.com**. Although this is an older version of PagePlus (the current version is 11), it is not restricted in any way and can be used indefinitely. The file size is 20MB, making it downloadable in a few minutes over a broadband connection, and in a couple of hours using a standard 56k dial-up modem.

Why not use a word processor instead?

To the uninitiated, it might seem that there's little to choose between a word processor and a specialist desktop-publishing program. Both types of software enable you to input text and format it in eye-catching ways and with both of them you can incorporate pictures and tables, but there the similarities end because the modes of operation are completely different.

The strength of a word processor is its ability to tackle linear documents, which are those where the words flow from page to page, adjusting their flow automatically as blocks of text are added or taken away. Although a word-processed document is often divided into chapters and sections by various kinds of headings, the text itself is a single file beginning on page one and

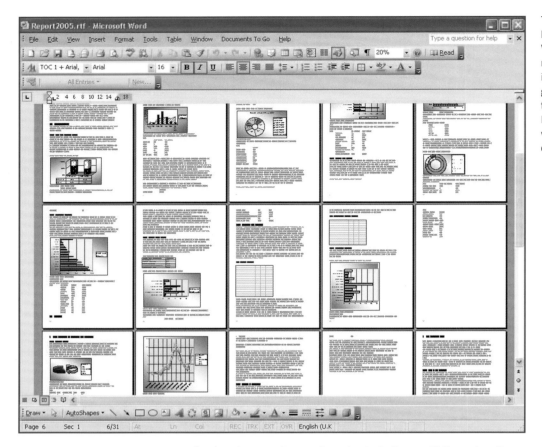

To prove it can be done, here's a long company report produced in Word 2003. The layout had to be restricted to a single column and it was extremely difficult to keep graphics on the same pages as the accompanying text and tables. Editing the finished report is virtually impossible without destroying the layout.

flowing down each page from top to bottom until it reaches the end. Any pictures or tables are treated as minor interruptions to the inevitable flow of text from start to finish.

The page-layout programs used in desktop publishing are very different. Instead of a continuous stream of words filling the entire publication, there are numerous shorter text files. Some of these are very short indeed and can be fitted into a single frame on a single page. Others are longer and can be made to flow from frame to frame over several pages. Each text file, or story as it is called in desktop publishing, can be edited independently. You may even remove an entire story and leave its encompassing frames in place without the problem of every other page flowing back to fill the gaps and ruining your carefully planned design. Imagine the problems of trying to create a newspaper in a word processor, when late-breaking news added to the front page would cause every other page to lose its shape.

Frames are central to desktop publishing because every object on a page, be it a text file, a photograph, a drawing or a table, must be in its own frame. Far from being restrictive, this is very liberating because you can move frames around a page, resize them, and even move them from page to page with complete freedom. Stories can begin on one page and be continued in another frame 20 pages later. If you add text to the opening frame, it will automatically flow into the later frame if necessary. Unlike word processing, desktop publishing is completely non-linear. The user decides exactly what is to appear on each page and where, and this makes the page the fundamental unit of design in desktop publishing, whereas in word processing it is the document itself.

Despite its inflexibility, a word processor is an incredibly useful productivity tool and there's no reason to choose anything else for personal projects, everyday business tasks and documents made up primarily of text, especially if they will be printed on an inkjet or laser printer. For any publication that involves a strong graphical element or the assembly of work from numerous contributors, or is destined for commercial printing, a dedicated page-layout program is essential.

Ten reasons to choose DTP

- Every item on a page is contained in a frame which can be moved, edited or removed without affecting any other frames.
- Stories can be contained in a single frame or allowed to flow between several frames.
- Frames do not have to appear in a 'logical' sequence. Text can flow from a later frame to an earlier one if necessary.
- Each frame acts as a mini page and can have its own settings for columns and margins without affecting any other frame.
- Underlying every page is an invisible master page which can carry information such as logos, background images and page numbers that you wish to be repeated on every page.
- Picture frames can have a more sophisticated range of adjustments and special effects than are available in a word processor, and each frame can be adjusted without affecting any other.
- The way that pictures and text interact can be finely controlled.
- Publications can be output in a form suitable for commercial printing using separations for each colour.
- A wide range of document formats is available including folded brochures, booklets and multi-sheet posters. You can leave the program to worry about which pages need to be printed upside down or in a special sequence.
- Multiple stories from any number of separate authors can be handled with ease.

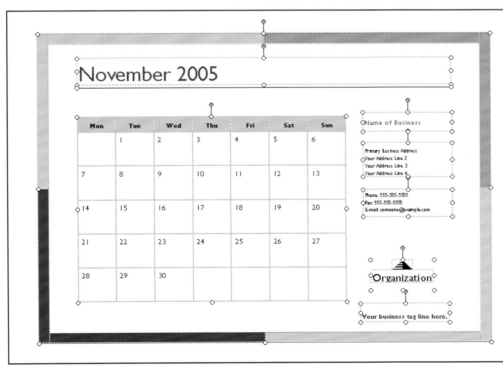

This calendar clearly demonstrates how frames allow for complete flexibility in design. It has eight separate frames (border, month name, calendar and five items of company information) which can all be moved and resized independently.

Planning a new publication

Desktop-publishing programs come with ready-made templates for publications that tie in with common home and business projects. Using templates can save a lot of repetitive work and there are times when using them is the only sensible way to proceed. It's great to be able to knock out a quick greetings card when you've forgotten somebody's birthday and all the shops are closed. You can personalise the card with your own message and change the graphic to one that's appropriate for the occasion, and the result will be a unique creation.

Different criteria apply to prestige projects such as reports, newsletters, brochures and catalogues. A template is unlikely to include every element you need or have everything laid out just the way you want it, so the template is best regarded as a starting point for further development. Even after making changes, your publication will not be unique and it's likely to have a similar look and feel to publications devised by other people using the same template. It's therefore important to understand how to design your own publications from scratch for those occasions when you really want to go to town with an original design, and for when no suitable template exists for the task you have in mind.

Before you begin, it's a good idea to rough out on paper what a typical page in the publication will look like in terms of the number of columns, the placement of graphics and the use of headers and footers. Consider too whether it will be bound and, if so, how. You may need to leave a wider margin along the bound edges, even if only a simple ring- or comb-binding system is used. All these things will influence the design of the master pages in your publication. The master pages contain the non-printing grids you'll use to position every frame, and they may also contain printable elements that repeat from page to page, such as headers, footers, page numbers and background images. Every page you create will be based on an underlying master page that acts as a design aid. Some publications use the same

However meagre your artistic talents, simple sketches like these will enable you to work out the number of columns and vertical divisions required on each page. Notice that some frames cut across two or three columns. This is perfectly acceptable.

master page for every page, but in others you'll use different master pages at different points in the publication.

You'll also need to know the size of paper the finished publication will be printed on and, if you're going to print it yourself, you'll need to consult the printer manual to find out exactly how much of the chosen paper size can be printed. Most printers cannot print to all four edges of every paper size so it's important to know the limitations of your printer if you want to avoid disappointment later. If the publication will be going out to a commercial print shop, seek advice on whether you need to leave space for trimming and, if so, how much.

This extract from a CD-based printer manual illustrates the device's unprintable margins when using three common paper sizes. It's worth making a note of your printer's limitations at all the paper sizes you are likely to use.

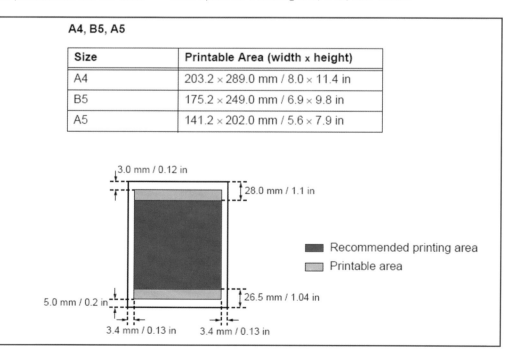

A4, B5, A5

Size	Printable Area (width x height)
A4	203.2 × 289.0 mm / 8.0 × 11.4 in
B5	175.2 × 249.0 mm / 6.9 × 9.8 in
A5	141.2 × 202.0 mm / 5.6 × 7.9 in

3.0 mm / 0.12 in
28.0 mm / 1.1 in
■ Recommended printing area
□ Printable area
5.0 mm / 0.2 in
26.5 mm / 1.04 in
3.4 mm / 0.13 in
3.4 mm / 0.13 in

Setting up master pages in Microsoft Publisher

In this step-by-step guide you'll set up a three-column, six-row grid for A4 paper. It will have two master pages: one for left-hand pages and another for those on the right. This is suitable for almost any community, business and club newsletter. The three-column format enables a flexible combination of frames spanning one, two or three columns to be used, and each column is wide enough to display a reasonable number of words at 9 and 10 point font sizes.

You'll also set up a simple page-numbering system at the bottom of each page, but you won't be formatting it at this stage. The newsletter will be stapled at the top left corner so there's no need to leave additional space for binding, but because some readers like to punch their own holes and collect newsletters in a ring binder, you'll add 4mm to the inner margins to facilitate this.

Start Microsoft Publisher 2003 and, on the opening screen, click Blank Publications in the task pane on the left. This displays a pictorial menu on the right-hand side of the screen, as shown here. Click on Full Page to create an A4-sized blank canvas. Although full pages are created as A4 by default, they can be changed to any other size through the File menu by clicking Page Setup. If you change the default paper size, it's important to do it before you create margins and guide lines, because changing the paper size throws these elements out of alignment.

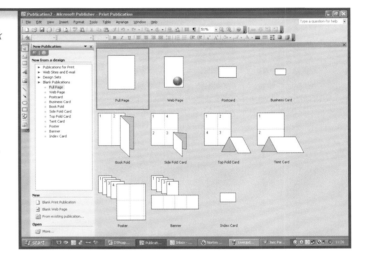

On the View menu, click Master Page, and then press function key F9 to zoom the page to actual size. F9 is a very useful key in Publisher because it switches instantly between the currently selected zoom level and 100%. Use the vertical scroll bar to bring the top edge of the page into view. On the Arrange menu, click Ruler Guides. You're going to use ruler guides to delineate the non-printable areas of the page. From the printer manual, these have been determined to be 3mm at the top, 5mm at the bottom and 3.4mm on either side. There are two ways of setting ruler guides: by dragging them out from one of the rulers and dropping them on the page, or by using the Format Ruler Guides option to specify an exact position for each guide. Start with the first method by dragging a guide from the top ruler to the 3mm position on the vertical ruler, then release the mouse button.

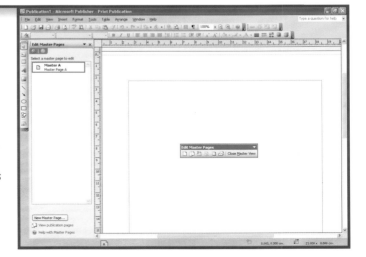

3

To make the positioning of the bottom ruler guide easier, use the zoom control on the standard toolbar to switch to 400% view, and then scroll down until you are looking at the bottom left corner of the page. The page length can now clearly be seen to be 29.7cm. The unprintable area is 5mm, so you need to drag a guide from the top ruler and position it at 29.2cm.

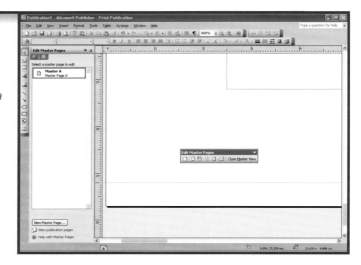

4

As you may have noticed, the guides snap to the divisions on the ruler. This makes it impossible to set the left-hand ruler guide at exactly 3.4mm because the closest division is at 3.5mm. One solution is to turn off the snapping effect, which can be accomplished using the Snap command on the Arrange menu, but it's faster and more accurate to do it as follows: open the Arrange menu and select Ruler Guides, followed by Format Ruler Guides. When the Ruler Guides dialogue box is displayed, select the Vertical tab and type 0.34cm as the guide position. Click Set. The page is 21cm wide so the right-hand ruler guide needs to be set at 21cm less 3.4mm, which is 20.66cm. Simply type this in and click the Set button again. Click OK to close the dialogue box and the guides will appear on the master page. To check that all four ruler guides are in place use the zoom control to select Whole Page view, or use the shortcut key combination Shift+Ctrl+L.

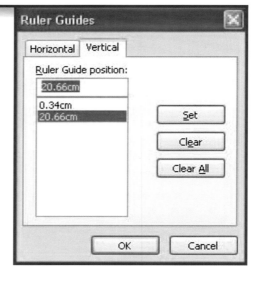

5

To set the margins and choose a grid design for the page, open the Arrange menu and click Layout Guides. When the Layout Guides dialogue box opens, select the Margin Guides tab and click Two-page master. The page diagram will then change to display two facing pages instead of a single page. Use the spinner controls to set the top, bottom and outside margins to 2cm. The inside margins need to be 4mm wider (for the benefit of readers who want to punch and bind) so type 2.4cm into the Inside panel instead of using the spinners. Don't click OK yet because doing so will close the dialogue box.

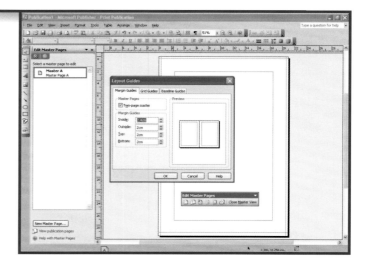

6

Click the Grid Guides tab and use the spinner controls to set the number of columns to 3. In this case the spinner controls are better than typing because as you use them, the changes are immediately reflected in the diagram. In the Row Guides section use the spinners to set the number of rows to 6. You'll notice that a space of 0.5cm is automatically added between the columns and rows. While the spacing is welcome between columns because it makes text easier to read, you don't really want it between rows because the row grid is only there to help you place pictures and frames with accuracy. Eliminate the row spacing by setting it at 0cm using its spinners.

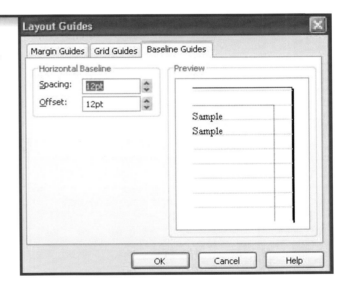

7

The third tab in the Layout Guides dialogue box is Baseline Guides. Click it now and take a look. Unlike the guides for rulers and margins, these are not displayed on the screen at all times because they are not intended to be used as positioning guides by the operator. If you choose to turn them on, baseline guides are used by Publisher itself to ensure that lines of text in adjacent columns stay in alignment by conforming to the spacing specified here. It doesn't really make sense to change the baseline grid until you know what size fonts you'll be using, so for now leave it at its default setting of 12 points. Click OK to close the dialogue box.

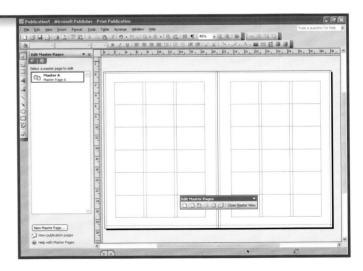

8

You can now see the effect of your changes displayed on the two-page master. If everything is in order, click Close Master View in the floating toolbar. This will leave you looking at a single page that is ready to have frames of text and pictures added to it. Bear in mind that none of the guides and grids you can see will appear on anything you print. They are simply there to help you compose your pages. Neither does the act of setting up the margins force you to stay within them. There's nothing to stop you using all the printable space within the area bounded by the ruler guides. Before you finish, use the Save As command on the File menu and choose to save your work as a template (not a publication) called A4grid3x6. Provided you save it in Publisher's Templates folder, it will appear in the Preview Gallery whenever you choose to create a new publication. You may now close Publisher.

PART 2 **Working with text**

You're already aware that text in a page-layout program has to be contained in frames, but how does it get there? In fact there are three main ways, and each has its own strengths in certain situations:

1. You can type it in to a frame. All the latest desktop-publishing programs have efficient text editors with built-in spelling checkers. In some of the programs there is also an autocorrection option that fixes common mistakes and typing errors, but you're unlikely to find a page-layout program with the same sophisticated synonym finders, grammar checkers and definition dictionaries as a word processor, and it's also very inconvenient having to keep creating a new text frame every time the one you're working on fills up. In general, you'll only type directly into a desktop-publishing program when you're adding short titles and captions or editing text imported from elsewhere.

2. You can create and save text using any word processor or text editor, and then load the saved file direct from disk into a text frame. This is the preferred way of working. Even if a contributor sends you a file in a format for which you don't have the program, such as WordPerfect or Microsoft Works, you can still use the file provided your desktop-publishing program can load that format. To be on the safe side, it's usual to ask contributors to submit work in one of the 'universal' formats such as plain text (where the filename ends in .TXT) or rich text format (file names ending in .RTF).

While it's fine to use all of the composition and correction tools that word processors provide for you, it's best to steer clear of any formatting options if you're typing specifically for use in a desktop-publishing program. Don't apply styles, colours, or fancy fonts. Don't use hanging indents, justification, section breaks or page breaks. Don't use bullets or auto-numbering (but you can indicate their presence by manually typing asterisks and numbers). Use bold and italic highlighting for emphasis if you must, but as a general rule leave other types of formatting to be applied as part of the desktop publishing process. If you are presented with heavily formatted files, try loading them into the program that created them and then stripping out the formatting by resaving the files as plain text.

3. You can copy text from any program running at the same time as your desktop publisher and paste it into a text frame. This is a tedious way of acquiring large amounts of text so it's usually reserved for cutting and pasting passages from reference works or websites. It's also useful if you receive work in a format that your desktop-publishing software cannot load. Simply load the file into another program, copy it from there and paste it into a text frame.

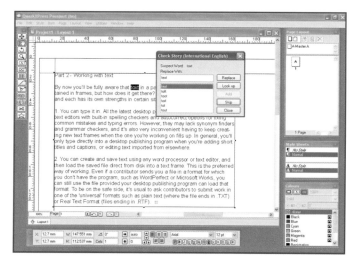

The only language tools in QuarkXpress are a spelling checker and a simple word count facility.

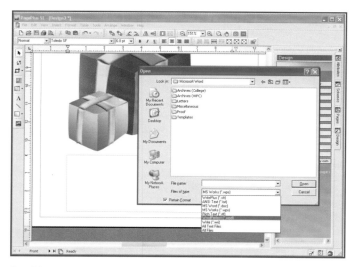

PagePlus can load proprietary files created in Word, Works, WordPerfect and Serif's own WritePlus, as well as files in any of the universal text formats.

What is a text frame?

A text frame, or text box as it is called in some programs, can be regarded as a miniature page that exists within a larger page and can be moved to any position within the larger page. To describe a text box in this way is no exaggeration because, like a normal page, it has its own fully adjustable margins, it can have multiple columns, and the text follows its formatting and justification rules.

When you place a block of text or a file into a text frame it is unlikely to fill the frame exactly. It's far more common for the text to fill only a part of the frame or to fill the entire frame but with an overflow that cannot be seen. In cases like these, there are several ways you can cope. If the overflow or underflow is relatively slight, you can probably adjust the size of the text box to make it fit, or you can edit the text to add or delete words until the length is suitable. If there is a major overflow and the text box cannot be made larger, you simply create another text box elsewhere in the publication – on the same page or on any other – and pipe the overflow into the second frame. If the overflow is not completely absorbed by the second frame you can go on linking further text frames until the entire story is accommodated. Another approach is to change the size of the font within the frame to make the text fit, but this is usually unsatisfactory because the text will be at odds with other fonts used in the same publication. However, it's a viable solution if the frame is meant to stand apart, such as an advertisement, special offer or table of contents.

This text box in QuarkXpress has been formatted to contain two columns. It also demonstrates how a text box can be governed by its own margin settings, which are independently adjustable on all four sides.

Create and use text frames

In order to practise using text frames you'll need some text to put in them. Any text will do provided it is unformatted and not full of superfluous line breaks, but the best sort of text for this purpose is *lorem ipsum* text. This is a passage of mangled Latin that begins with the words *lorem ipsum*. It has the advantage of filling up text frames and breaking from line to line in much the same way as English yet, because it is incomprehensible, you can concentrate on the layout without getting hung up on what the words mean.

Users of Adobe InDesign can fill any text frame with *lorem ipsum* text simply by right-clicking on the frame and selecting Fill with Placeholder Text. Users of other programs will find that a Google search for 'Lorem Ipsum' turns up plenty of sources on the web, with one of the most useful being **www.lipsum.com**. There you can read the history of *lorem ipsum*, and generate as much of it as you require. Before working through the steps outlined below, generate 20 paragraphs of *lorem ipsum* text. Select the text and copy it, then paste it into a text editor or word processor. Once it's there, save a copy on disk using the filename `Lorem.rtf`.

Start Publisher 2003. In the step-by-step guide to creating master pages (see p.51.), you created and saved a template called A4grid3x6.pub. To load this, click Templates in the task pane on the left, and then click A4grid3x6 in the Preview pane on the right. If you don't have the template saved on disk, you can quickly make a similar document by clicking Blank Publications and then selecting Full Page. When the page appears on screen, open the Arrange menu and click Layout Guides. In the Layout Guides dialogue box click the Grid Guides tab. Change the Columns setting to 3 and the Rows setting to 6. Click OK.

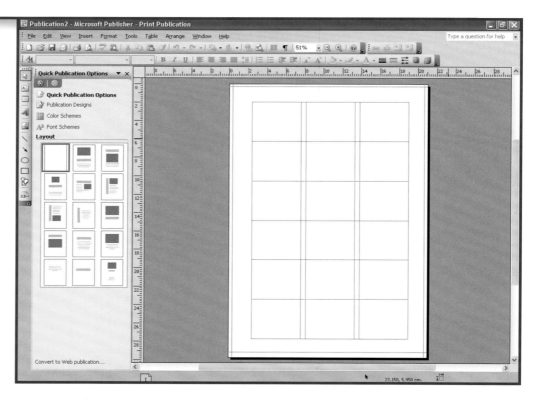

2

To add some blank pages to your publication, open the Insert Menu and click Page. In the Insert Page dialogue box, type 3 as the number of new pages, then click OK. You'll now see four icons (miniature pages) at the bottom of the screen. These represent the four pages in your publication and you can jump quickly to any page by clicking its icon. You may also move forwards or backwards one page at a time by holding down the Ctrl key and using Page Down or Page Up.

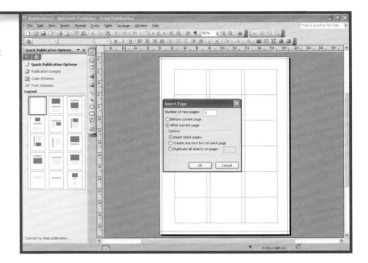

3

Click the Page 1 icon to ensure that the first page is selected, and then close the task pane by clicking the X in its top right corner. Press F9 to zoom to 100% view. Click the Text Box icon on the Objects toolbar (the vertical toolbar docked on the left of the screen), and you'll see the screen cursor change from a pointer to a cross-hair.

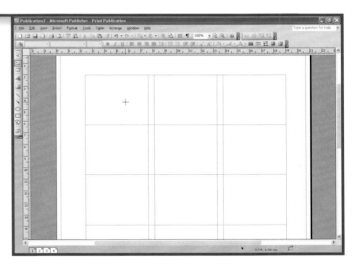

4

Click anywhere on the screen and a small text box will appear. This box can be resized and reshaped by grabbing any of its eight 'handles' (the hollow circles) and dragging them into position. To move the box, hover the cursor over its dotted boundary line until the cursor turns into a four-headed arrow. You can then hold down the left mouse button and drag the entire box to a new position before releasing the mouse button and dropping the box. Use a combination of these techniques to place the box over the first two grid elements in column 1. You'll notice that the text box snaps to the grid lines.

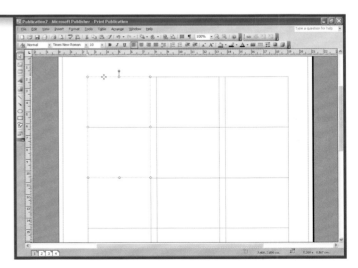

⑤ *Open the Insert menu and click Text File. In the Insert Text dialogue box, select your Lorem.rtf sample file or any other file of plain text, and then click OK. The text will fill the box and you'll then see this message asking if you want the remaining text to be automatically flowed into the rest of the document. Click No. Once the dialogue box drops out of sight the text is quickly spell-checked and, since it's in Latin, it is all underlined in red. To remove this annoyance, open the Tools menu, click Spelling, then click Hide Spelling Errors.*

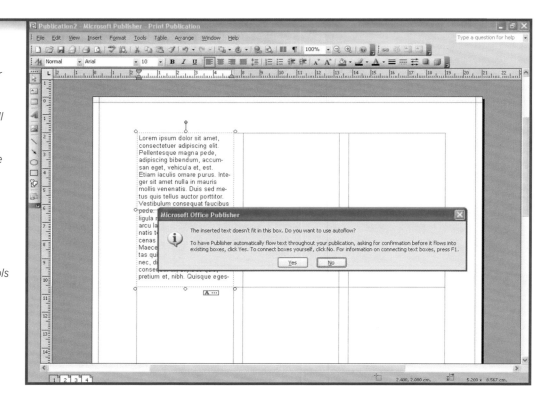

⑥ *Use the zoom control or press Shift+Ctrl+L to switch to whole page view. Beneath the text box is an icon containing the letter A followed by three dots. This is the overflow icon that tells you there is more text in the story than can be displayed in the text box. Grab the centre handle at the bottom of the text box and resize the box until it fills the first column in the grid. More text flows in to fill the bigger text box, but the presence of the overflow icon warns that there's still more text to be placed.*

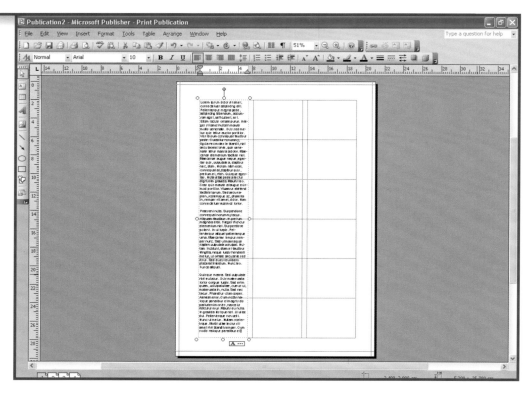

7

Create a second text box and place it so that it occupies all of column 2. When you do this, you may like to try an alternative way of creating text boxes. Instead of clicking to place a small box and then moving and resizing it, locate the cross-hair cursor where you want the top left corner of the box to be, and then hold down the left mouse button and drag out a box of exactly the shape and size you desire. When you release the mouse button, the box is created. If it isn't in exactly the right position you can make fine adjustments using the sizing handles. With the new text box in place and ready to accept overflow text, it now needs to be linked to the first text box. To do this, click on the text box in column 1 to select it, and then locate the Connect Text Boxes toolbar. By default, this is positioned to the right of the standard toolbar, but the screenshot shows it floating over the document.

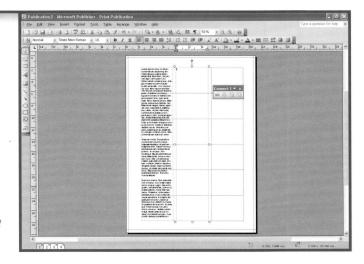

8

Click the Create Text Box Link icon (the chain on the left of the toolbar) and then move the cursor over the text box in the second column. You'll notice it has changed to a jug pouring letters. Click to fill the second box with text. When this has been done, the overflow icon moves to the bottom of the second text box to indicate that there is still more text to be placed, and a new icon with a green arrow is displayed at the top of the text box to indicate that this is a continuation box and not the start of the story.

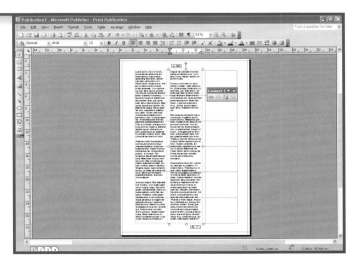

9

Text doesn't have to flow in an unbroken stream from column to column and page to page. To see how text can flow between pages, click on the Page 3 icon at the bottom of the screen and then create a new text box somewhere on page 3. Switch back to page 1 and click on the second text box. Click the Create Text Box Link icon, then switch back to page 3 and pour the text from the jug into the text box you've just placed there.

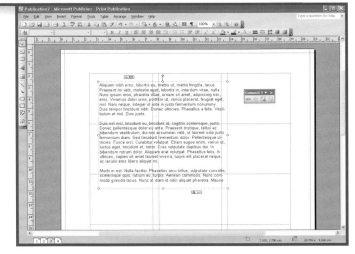

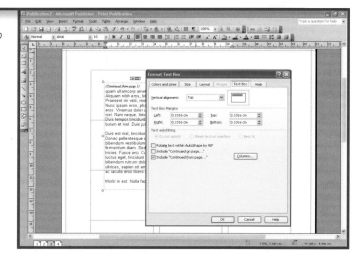

When a story is split over disconnected pages, the reader needs to be kept informed about where the story starts, and where it goes to if it jumps to a distant page. You could type this information yourself, but then you'd have to revise the page numbers every time a text box was moved to a new location. It's far better to format discontinuous text boxes to display their own continuity tags. To see this in action, right-click on the page 3 text box and select Format Text Box. When the Format Text Box dialogue box appears, click the Text Box tab, then tick the option labelled Include 'Continued from page…'. When you click OK, a message will appear at the top of the text box saying 'Continued from page 1'. Now switch to page 1 and use a similar technique to create a 'Continued on page 3' message at the end of text box 2. If you ever move the text box on page 3 to another page, the message on page 1 will automatically update itself to reflect the change.

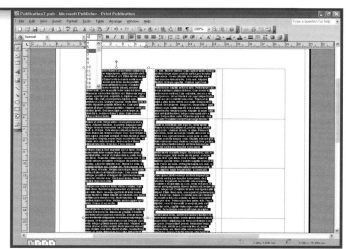

The two text boxes on page 1 and the text box on page 3 together constitute a single story, and it is therefore possible to make changes to the text formatting in all three boxes simultaneously. To see this in action, click on either of the page 1 text boxes, and then open the Edit menu and click Select All (or use the shortcut key Ctrl+A instead). With the text in all three boxes now selected, use the drop-down Font size selector on the formatting toolbar to change the font size to 6 points. To check that the font size has changed throughout the story, go to page 3 and confirm that the text there has also been reduced to 6 points.

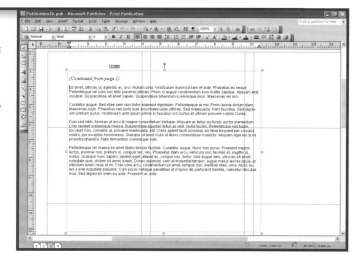

You will probably find that, at its new point size, the entire story now fits within the three text boxes without any overflow. If this is the case, when you click on the page 3 text box there will be no overflow icon at the bottom. There will still be a continuation icon at the top, pointing back to page 1 where the text originated, and it's worth remembering that these icons are more than merely informative: if you click on one of them it will take you immediately to its linked text box without all the fuss of navigating via the page icons at the bottom of the screen. Try it now by clicking the backwards-facing green arrow at the top of text box 3 to jump straight to text box 2 on page 1.

PART 2 Working with pictures and other objects

Pictures enhance almost any publication. While text appeals more to the intellect than the eye and has to be read before you can appreciate it, pictures have an immediate visual impact that entices viewers into the rest of the page. Apart from their impact, some types of pictures, such as the diagrams in an instruction manual or the photographs in a holiday brochure, are essential when they illustrate something that is difficult to convey in words but there are other types of picture that serve a very different function. Items such as logos, geometrical designs and clip art may not carry any essential meaning but they add colour and drama to a publication, break up forbiddingly long sections of text and make a publication look more interesting and approachable.

Sourcing pictures

The word 'picture' is shorthand for any type of graphical embellishment, be it an original bitmap or vector drawing produced on a computer, a photograph, a piece of clip art, or an item of printed artwork scanned into electronic format. Original photographs you've taken for yourself or which have been supplied by a contributor are a primary source, and by using these you can at least be sure readers haven't seen the same pictures before. Images captured on a digital camera can be imported straight from the camera or stored on hard disk until needed. Photographs from conventional film cameras can be imported after scanning them with a flatbed scanner.

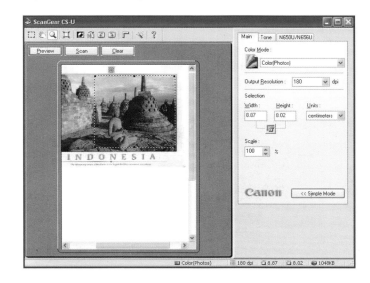

When scanning pictures from printed material, you get the chance to scan only the parts you need, and at the right resolution (if you're outputting to a desktop printer, this is 150–300dpi). If you're submitting work to a commercial print shop, ask the printer for guidance about scan settings.

Clip art seems to be included with almost every program you buy these days: office suites; drawing, painting and charting software; and page-layout programs themselves. Here's some of the clip art included with PageMaker 7.

If you don't have any original images, then photos from commercial sources are readily available, but usually at stiff prices in terms of fixed fees up front or royalties based on how the images will be used. Unless you're producing publications for sale, you probably won't want to pay the charges associated with using picture libraries and commercial image vendors, but there are plenty of places you can get hold of free photographs and illustrations if you're prepared to seek them out. Start by looking in the program folders on your hard disk where you may find clip art that was installed along with the programs. Also look on the CDs you installed the programs from, where additional clip art is often provided.

Picture collections on CD are available, and once you've bought a disc you can use its contents without restriction or further payment. Be careful, however: the images on some picture discs are samples and you're expected to pay royalties when you use them.

On the web, your first port of call for free photographs and illustrations should be **www.flickr.com/creativecommons**. Here you'll find hundreds of thousands of original graphics which are protected under Creative Commons licences. For many of them, all you need do when you use them is credit the creator; others are free to use but only for non-commercial purposes. Creative Commons licences come in several flavours, but all the images are clearly labelled so it's difficult to go wrong. Another source of Creative Commons images is **http://openphoto.net**, where there is a neat visual index to help you find what you're looking for. You can find out more about Creative Commons licences at **http://creativecommons.org**.

At Flickr, you can search for keywords or browse themed collections of pictures, while filtering the search to find only those pictures with Creative Commons licences.

iStockphoto, you can choose from around 700,000 cheap but often excellent royalty-free images.

If you're prepared to pay a small amount for your images, **www.istockphoto.com** is a photo library that has images for under US$5, royalty free.

Wherever you acquire images, check up on the terms and conditions of use, especially if you intend to use them in commercial publications. Images are covered by the law of copyright and you cannot assume that all images are free to use, even privately.

Incorporating pictures in a publication

As with adding text to a publication, there's more than one way of adding pictures, but because of the size of some images (particularly photographs) pictures are not treated in the same way as text after they've been added. In Adobe InDesign and PageMaker, pictures are added using the Place command on the

While it is possible to scan pictures directly into a publication, it's usually better to scan using your favourite image-editing program where you will be able to tweak the images with greater ease.

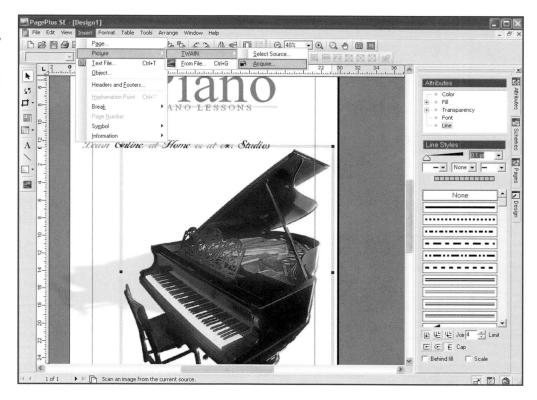

File menu. What gets placed on screen is a low resolution version of the original picture that is easy to manipulate and fast to update, but the original picture remains on disk and is required at print time. This means that all original pictures must accompany a saved publication when it is sent away for printing.

Other programs, notably Microsoft Publisher, assume when you import a picture that it will become part of the publication and will not necessarily be stored separately on disk. This is called embedding, and makes publications easier to manage, but it also causes file sizes to escalate alarmingly if a great many pictures are used. Once pictures are in place in Publisher, you can convert them singly or all at the same time into links, which you'll definitely need to do if you intend to have them printed commercially. In PagePlus 11, you get the choice of embedding or linking when you import a picture, and the program suggests you choose embedding for pictures under 256kB in size.

Formatting and laying out pictures

Once a picture is inserted in a publication it is automatically framed, and this frame can be moved around just like a text box. The picture can be sized within the frame, or you can retain the picture at its original size and use the frame as a sort of window onto the picture, revealing only the parts that are of interest. The effect is similar to cropping the picture but without the destructive effects. The frame is, of course, invisible when printed, but if you want to add a decorative frame or border you can. You can also add margins both inside and outside the frame. Inside the frame they distance the picture from its decorative border if it has one, while outside they distance the picture from the surrounding text.

Pictures can be slotted into convenient gaps between text

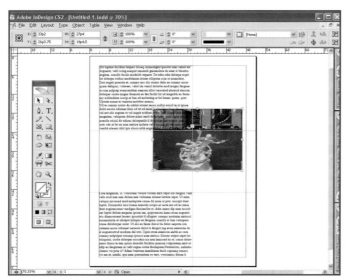

This picture is being slotted into a gap between two text frames in InDesign, but it's often easier to drop a picture onto a text frame and flow the text around it.

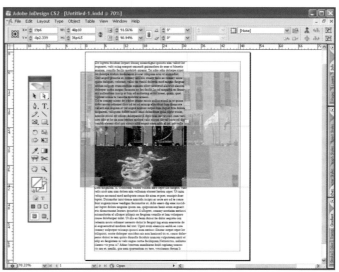

Panning an underlying photograph to determine exactly which section of it will be displayed in the picture frame.

frames, or you can place them on top of text frames and then cause the text to flow around them in various ways. Text flow is just one of the formatting controls you can apply to pictures. Others depend on the type of picture you're using. Photographs, for example, can have their brightness and contrast adjusted, borders and backgrounds can be added to any type of picture, and clip art elements can be re-coloured to suit other graphics on the same page without having to load them into a separate graphics program.

Sometimes you need to keep a particular picture close to a piece of text that refers to it. If the text flows elsewhere during editing, you want the picture to move with it. These so-called anchored or inline pictures are especially useful for placing small images and special symbols within a line of text. You will have seen examples of these in computer manuals and other instruction books. It's also possible to have an inline picture move with its linked text but be displayed between the lines rather than within them. As a general rule, restrict your use of inline pictures to those occasions when you genuinely need them, and take advantage of the greater control you are permitted when using pictures in floating frames.

Often you know you'll need a graphic at a particular point in a publication, but you don't yet have the picture to hand. Because this is such a common occurrence, all page-layout programs have a facility to place an empty picture frame to act as a place marker at a position where a picture will later be added. The place marker can be formatted exactly like a picture so that text flows around it in an appropriate manner, and the actual picture can be inserted at any time before printing without disturbing the flow of the rest of the publication.

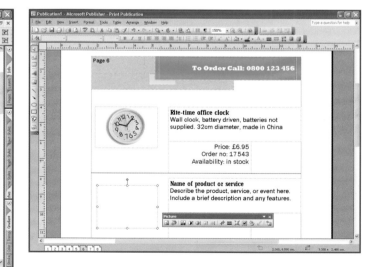

The fastest way to insert an inline or anchored graphic in most page-layout programs is to paste it into position exactly where it is required within the text, and then to format it appropriately.

In this catalogue, a place-holding picture frame has been allocated for the next item on the page. The presence of the Picture toolbar next to the frame is an indication that even empty picture frames can be formatted.

Using pictures in Microsoft Publisher

By now you should be familiar with master pages and how to use text boxes in Microsoft Publisher, so before you work through the steps outlined below, create an A4 sample document with two columns of text taking up the entire page. Fill the columns with *lorem ipsum* text, or any text file of your own, and save the publication as Picsample.pub. You should also select one of your own photographs, or one of the samples that comes with Windows, and save a copy of it using the filename Mypic.jpg.

❶

Start Publisher 2003 and load Picsample.pub. *On the Insert menu, select Picture and then click From File. Navigate to where you stored Mypic.jpg and select it. Click the Insert button to add the picture to the publication. The picture will be placed on top of the document – if it is a large picture it might completely obscure the page – but this is easily rectified by grabbing one of the corner sizing handles and dragging it towards the opposite corner until the picture is roughly the width of a single column.*

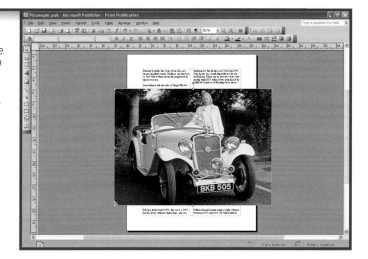

❷

Drag the picture off the page and drop it somewhere in the grey workspace area. You are now going to insert a piece of clip art from the collection included with Publisher, but before you do so you must click outside the picture frame you've just created to deselect it. If you fail to do this, the clip art will replace Mypic.jpg *instead of accompanying it. On the Insert menu, select Picture and then click Clip Art. The Clip Art task pane will open on the left of the screen. Type 'archery' into the Search panel and click Go. When you've found the target graphic shown here, click to add it to the page. It will be centred on the page. If the Picture toolbar obscures the document, move it out of the way.*

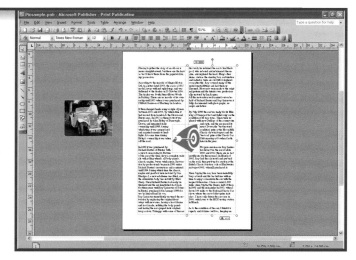

3

You can now drag the clip art picture into position so that it straddles the two columns a couple of centimetres from the bottom of the page. Position Mypic.jpg centrally about a quarter of the way down the page. If you have problems placing these pictures exactly in the centre, it's because they're snapping to either the column guides or the marks on the ruler. In this case, turn off snapping by selecting the Snap option on the Arrange menu, and then remove the ticks from Ruler Marks and Guides. Zooming in to 400% will also assist in accurate placement, and if you have a mouse with a centre wheel you can zoom quickly to any size by holding down the Ctrl button while rolling the wheel. Final fine adjustments can be made using the cursor control keys to 'nudge' the picture in any direction.

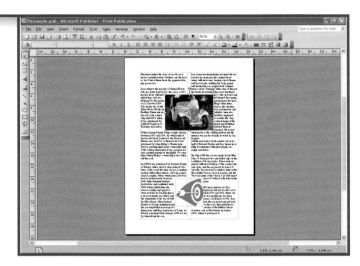

4

Whenever a picture frame is selected, the Picture toolbar should appear. If yours has disappeared, deselect the picture then reselect it to make the toolbar reappear. If you still can't see it, check to see that it is not docked at the top of the screen with the other toolbars. Almost every type of formatting action for pictures and picture frames can be applied using this toolbar. The first two icons from the left are for importing pictures from files or a scanner. If you use either of these, the new picture will replace the currently selected picture, in the same frame and at the same scale. Try it now if you have another picture on disk or on your scanner. The five controls in the next group are all concerned with adjusting the picture. The first controls the picture's colour and the next four govern contrast and brightness. The available colour settings are Automatic (i.e. the original colour), Grayscale, Black and White, and Washout. Try them now to see how they affect Mypic.jpg.

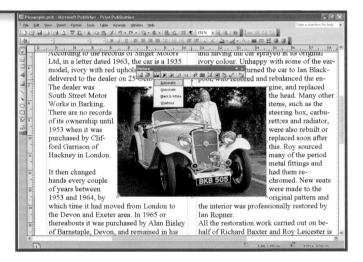

5

When you've finished experimenting with colours, set the colour to Automatic and press Ctrl+C to copy the picture. Now switch from the page you're working on to the master page by clicking Master Page on the View menu (or use the Ctrl+M shortcut). On the Master page, press Ctrl+V to paste a copy of your picture, then move the picture a few centimetres to one side. Use the colour control on the Picture toolbar to set the picture to Grayscale and Washout, then click the Close Master View button to return to your page. As you can now see, the washed-out picture on the master page shows through the current page, and text flows over it rather than around it because text only flows around objects on the same page. Attaching pictures to the master page is a useful way of creating artistic effects and watermarks.

6

Remove the washed-out version of the picture from the master page, and then return to the main page. The next tool on the toolbar is the Crop control, which allows you to display a selected portion from a larger picture but does not actually remove any information from the file stored on disk. Next to this is the Line/Border style control, with which you can add simple frames to your pictures. The presets work well on pictures with white or pale backgrounds, but for darker backgrounds like the picture used here, click the More Lines option for access to the sophisticated framing features available on the Colors and Lines tab of the Format Picture dialogue box.

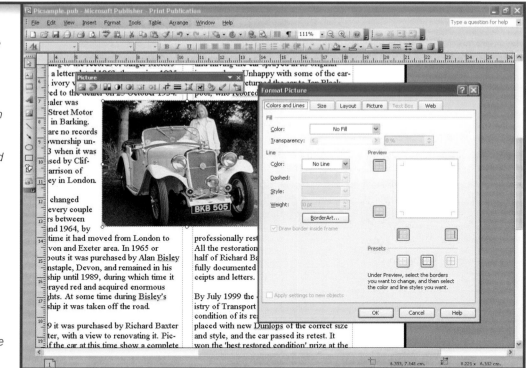

7

The line controls work very much like the border and line options you'll be familiar with from your word processor, but for something fancier click the Border Art button. This displays the dialogue box shown here where you can choose from 164 different border styles. The one selected is Basic…Wide Midline. If none of the built-in borders meets your needs you can make your own by clicking the Create Custom button. You'll then be asked to choose a graphic (one of your own or a piece of clip art) and Publisher will turn it into a border for you.

8

The next control on the Picture toolbar compresses pictures to save space on disk. The required operations can be carried out on a single picture or on every picture in a publication. If you are creating a publication for the web, then compression is well worth carrying out because by changing the resolution to Web/Screen you reduce the pixels in each picture to 96dpi, which can result in an enormous space saving with no apparent loss of quality. If you choose Print resolution, then pictures are reduced to 200dpi, but this is unlikely to save much space with digital camera pictures because the majority of cameras are preset to 72dpi or 144dpi anyway. It will make a difference to scanned pictures, and especially to those scanned from slides at resolutions of up to 2700dpi. You may also choose to discard the unused portion of cropped pictures, which if you have been cropping down to small sizes can save a lot of disk space. Reducing the resolution of pictures in a publication will have an impact on final print quality so be sure to keep a copy of the uncompressed versions of all your files in case you need them.

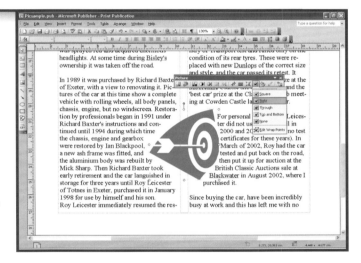

9

In print publications, when you place pictures on top of text boxes the default action is for text to flow around them, but you can change this relationship by using the Text Wrapping control on the Picture toolbar. When you're working on web publications, text cannot be made to flow around pictures so the Text Wrapping control does not appear on the Picture toolbar. To see the text wrapping options in action, scroll down the page and zoom in on the clip art graphic you placed near the bottom. Click the Text Wrapping button and you'll see that Square is selected by default, which results in the text following the rectangular outline of the frame, rather than the shape of the picture itself. To make the text wrap to the picture, click Tight. If you see a message asking if it's OK for Publisher to create a new text boundary, click Yes.

10

With most pictures the Through option is the same as Tight, but with some irregularly shaped graphics it allows the text to get closer to the picture. The Top and Bottom option forces text to stop above the picture and continue below it, which is often desirable when the picture covers a single column of text but is unsuitable for a graphic like this one which straddles two or more columns. With None selected the graphic sits on top of the text and obscures the words directly beneath it. The Edit Wrap Points selection creates a flexible frame which initially follows the contours of the picture but which can then be adjusted so that text flows around the wrap points and not around the picture itself.

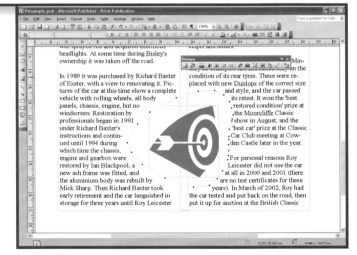

Next to the Text Wrapping control is the Format Picture control. When you click on this, a tabbed dialogue box appears through which all of the adjustments on the Picture toolbar are available, plus a few more. On the Picture tab, for example, is a Recolor button, which allows you to change the colour of a picture. With a simple shape like this one it's easy to see the advantages of colour changing, because if a graphic is not available in the colour you want, you can create your own. It's also useful with photographs when it can be used to create special effects similar to what photographers called duotones. Try it and see (dark colours work best).

Second from the right on the Picture toolbar is a button that enables you to redefine any single colour in a picture as a transparent area. One application for this is with pictures such as studio portraits where a foreground subject is placed against a plain background. Making the background transparent allows you to wrap text to the outline of the subject instead of to the frame, and it is also useful for adding transparency to web graphics so they appear to float over the background. It works only with bitmap images so you can't try it out with your sample piece of clip art, but you can apply it to Mypic.jpg. The remaining icon on the Picture toolbar is the reset button, but be warned before you use it that it resets every change you've made to a picture since your most recent save, so in most cases it's preferable to correct mistakes by selecting them from the list attached to the Undo arrow on the main toolbar.

File formats explored

You now know enough to start creating your own publications, and in Part 3 there are plenty of practical examples to help you build your skills. There's only one item to be considered first, which is the sometimes tricky question of which file formats to use in your publications. This is seldom a problem when using ordinary office applications, because the only time you need to choose a file format is when saving your work; and the only time you don't use the default file type is when you want to share files with somebody who doesn't necessarily use the same programs as you.

In desktop publishing, things are very different: a page-layout program is basically an assembly line where files created in other programs are the components. You need to know something about the strengths and weaknesses of each type of file if you are to remain in control of your publication. Broadly there are three categories of file:

● Files containing text and pictures for inclusion in your publications
● The native file format of your page layout software
● Output files for printing

Text formats

Text files are the least problematic to deal with. Text can be imported directly from certain proprietary word-processor formats and from any of the universal text formats that can be produced by every word processor. Every page-layout program can read Microsoft Word files and most of them can read WordPerfect files,

QuarkXpress 6.1 is fairly typical in terms of the range of text files it can import.

but beyond these you won't find many word processors directly supported. If you go through the process of opening a file in your page-layout program you'll be able to see which file types can be directly loaded.

For word processor formats that are not well supported – and these include Lotus AmiPro, XyWrite and Microsoft Works – make sure that their files are saved in RTF or TXT formats. This is a simple matter of using the Save As command on the word processor's file menu. You can turn HTML or XML files into text files in the same way after loading them into your word processor, though some page-layout programs, including Microsoft Publisher, can also read them directly.

Bear in mind if you use an old version of a word processor that file formats are sometimes changed when new versions of a program are released. WordPerfect files, for example, have been revised twice, and only the most recent WPD format is generally acceptable. The way to handle older non-compatible formats is, as before, to save the files as text.

Bitmap graphics

Graphics files contain either bitmap or vector data. Bitmap data consists of tiny coloured squares or pixels. Bitmap files are produced by scanners and digital cameras, though it is also possible to create original bitmap art using a paint program. The main difference between bitmaps and vectors is that vector graphics can be scaled to any size without losing picture quality, while bitmap images look their best at or below their actual size, and the more you enlarge or zoom in on them, the rougher their appearance becomes.

The three bitmap formats you'll need most are TIFF, JPEG and GIF. Incidentally, TIF and JPG are sometimes written instead of TIFF and JPEG, but the files are the same. TIFF is the best format to use for desktop publishing because it is lossless. In other words, a TIFF image contains every piece of information that was gathered by the scanner or camera that captured it. A JPEG version of the same image is 'lossy' because some of the original information is discarded in order to make the file size smaller.

Despite the technical superiority of TIFF files, you may find the smaller size of JPEG files easier to manage, especially if your computer is short of memory or disk space, and sometimes you don't have the choice, as when using a digital camera that can only store JPEG images. TIFF and JPEG files are both capable of storing full-colour images using millions of colours, and the colour information can be in RGB or CMYK format, which makes them suitable for any type of desktop publishing. It's usual to work on screen with pictures saved in RGB mode while designing a publication, then to convert the pictures to CMYK before sending them for commercial printing. Although it is possible to compress a TIFF file to save space, you can't make it anything like as small as a JPEG. This is because no information is discarded when a TIFF file is compressed.

GIF files are tiny compared with TIFF and JPEG files. Although

When importing text, check to see if there are options that will make subsequent editing easier, such as removing unwanted spaces and turning plain quote marks into typographer's quotes. These are the available options in Adobe InDesign.

This bitmap seems to offer a naturalistic rendition of shapes and colours, but zoom in too far on those balloons and you start to see the underlying grid of pixels.

This rather extreme example shows the inadvisability of saving photographic images in GIF format.

GIF files can display up to 16.8 million colours, a single GIF image can contain a maximum of only 256 different colours, so they're not suitable for photographic work. They are ideal for use on the web because their small size makes them fast to load, and they can include a transparent colour to allow web backgrounds to show through. It's also possible to animate a GIF file by including several images in the same file. Web browsers then display them in sequence by cycling through the separate images like a short strip of film. If you include an animated GIF in a print publication you see only the first image.

Another bitmap format you might come across is the BMP format devised by Microsoft for use by Windows. Like TIFF, it's a lossless format, but it can only contain RGB colour information. There's nothing you can do with BMP that you can't do with TIFF, so always convert BMP files to TIFF by loading pictures into an image-editing program and using the Save As option.

Vector graphics

Vector graphics are not built up of coloured pixels. Instead, the data in a vector file is defined mathematically as lines and curves. Think of a vector file as a set of instructions telling you how to draw a picture, rather than the picture itself. Because the instructions are the same regardless of how big the picture is, a vector graphic looks good at any size from postage stamp to poster.

Vector images like this cartoon hot rod may look indistinguishable from hand-drawn artwork, but strip away the rendered surfaces and underneath you see the geometrical framework that supports them.

Vector graphics are created by drawing programs such as Adobe Illustrator, CorelDRAW and AutoCAD. Each of these programs has its own file format but for use in desktop publishing you should save files in Encapsulated PostScript (EPS) format, or export them as bitmaps at the size you will be using them. Although EPS is a vector format, an EPS picture file may also contain an optional preview image in bitmap format. This allows programs that can't display EPS files to at least display an approximation of the picture. The complete vector data is used for printing.

The only other vector formats you need for desktop publishing are the Windows MetaFile (WMF) and Enhanced Windows Metafile (EMF) formats. Most clip art is distributed in WMF format. Save your own vector files as EPS if your page-layout program can load them, or use EMF and WMF if it can't. The EPS format is not only more sophisticated than either of the Windows Metafile formats, it is also fully compatible with Apple Mac hardware and software.

Clip art in WMF format keeps its looks however large you scale it.

DTP software and printing formats

Every desktop-publishing program uses a proprietary file format to store publications. Even the three page-layout programs made by Adobe can't open each other's files (although InDesign deserves an honourable mention for being able to open files created in PageMaker and QuarkXpress versions 3 and 4). File incompatibility is not really a problem unless you intend to work co-operatively on laying out a publication, in which case all concerned should use the same software.

Once a publication has been completed, it can be saved in a format other than the internal format of the layout program and sent for printing. The two most useful formats are Encapsulated PostScript (EPS), which has already been introduced as a vector file format, and Adobe's Portable Document Format (PDF). Of the two, EPS has been around longer and is acceptable to every commercial printer. PDF is not yet universally accepted despite being a more versatile format. Be guided by your printer as to which format you should use.

One advantage of PDF files is that they can be displayed on screen using a simple program such as Adobe Reader, or on the web using a browser add-in, and their on-screen appearance exactly matches their appearance in print, regardless of the computer and operating system used. Another advantage is that a PDF file can contain every text and pictorial element of a publication in a single file, whereas a publication in EPS format will be split over several files.

Every page-layout program can produce EPS files, and most can produce PDF files. For those that can't (such as Microsoft Publisher), you can use a supplementary printer driver to generate PDF file output.

If you are sending a multiple-page document to a commercial printer and they can't accept a PDF file, the best option would be to send a single Postscript file rather than separate EPS files for each page (especially true if there are a great many pages to the document).

Regardless of which format you choose, you will need to consult your printer for advice about how to generate the files. Not only are there three variants of the PostScript language (Level 1, Level 2 and PostScript 3), but there are also numerous options to be selected when generating the files. Your printer will be able to tell you which settings to use for issues such as crop marks, bleed marks, font substitution and halftone screening.

A single PDF file can contain a book with hundreds or even thousands of pages of text, complete with illustrations, and it can be read with the free Adobe Reader software.

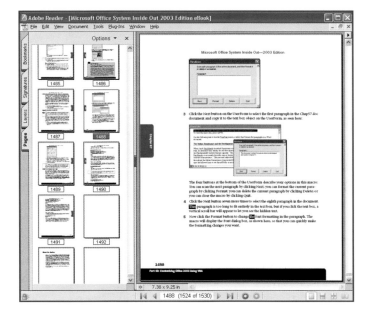

PART **3** **DTP projects**

PART 3 Design and template tutorial

Creating short documents of all kinds in Microsoft Publisher is a breeze thanks to the program's built-in designs. In Publisher, a design refers to an advanced type of template with a high degree of automation and built-in wizards help to simplify things still further. Of course, Publisher can use ordinary templates too, and these work very much like the ones you'll be familiar with from your word processor, but most of the templates supplied with Publisher are actually designs. The only ones that are not designs are the 11 blank publications, plus any that you've downloaded from the Microsoft Office website or created for yourself by saving existing publications as templates for future work.

As a general rule, whenever you start a new project in Publisher, look for a ready-made design before wasting valuable time building the publication from scratch. After using a design, if the end product is not exactly what you want, you can make whatever changes are necessary using the techniques with text and pictures described in Part 2.

The design for folded greetings cards contains 300 ready-made examples, but by substituting your own pictures and messages you can create unique cards for any occasion.

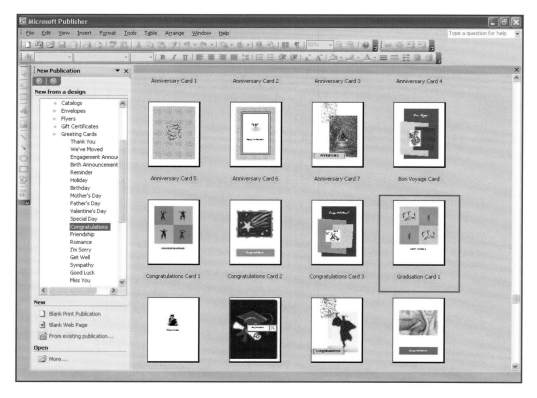

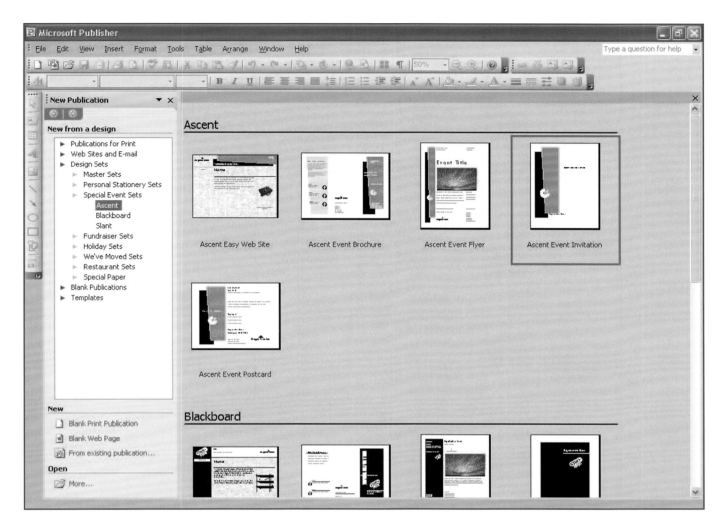

When looking for designs, delve into Publications for Print or Web sites and E-mail to find documents listed by type, or into Design Sets if you want to see documents grouped by appearance.

The designs suitable for business documents are grouped into Master sets, with a set being a collection of related documents all matching in terms of their colour, typography, layout and decorative style. In all there are 45 design sets for business, each with a unique appearance, and within each design set up to 36 different types of document can be produced, ranging from business cards and calendars to time bills and weekly record sheets. Business documents are often photocopied or faxed. It's a good idea to avoid certain colours and combinations: yellow doesn't show up, red copies as black (so avoid black type on a red background or vice versa), etc.

Other design sets exist for personal stationery and events such as fundraising and moving home.

The benefits of using design templates

When you elect to base a document on a design, a number of things happen automatically. First, a new publication is created, and then all the relevant settings are pre-configured for the chosen type of publication. These include page and paper sizes, margins and folding options. If the publication spans several pages, all the necessary additional pages are generated, and then the entire publication is filled with place-holding text and pictures. If the document includes names, addresses or

Microsoft Office Professional Edition 2003

Installation Error: File not Found

A required installation file P4561402.CAB could not be found

Original Installation Source Required:

If you installed Microsoft Office Professional Edition 2003 from a CD, please insert your CD. If you installed Microsoft Office Professional Edition 2003 over your computer network, please browse to the installation source on your network. Once you have located your installation source, click OK.

Browse

OK   Cancel

company information, all these items are completed for you based on personal and company information you supply. Control of the publication then passes to you. In the task pane on the left of the screen are four sets of options, through which you can:

● Make changes that are specific to the publication. These vary according to the type of document being produced. For example, in a calendar you can change the month and year, and choose whether or not to include a list of key dates.
● Change the design from the one you initially selected to any of the others offered by Publisher. In some cases there are hundreds to choose from.
● Change the colour scheme of the entire publication. There are 66 different colour combinations to choose from or you can define your own.
● Change the font scheme for the entire publication. Each of the 32 pre-defined schemes uses different font and style combinations or you can define your own.

The use of designs means that before you start working on text and frames, you can create tens of thousands of unique variations on a single document type simply by mixing and matching different combinations of designs, colours and font schemes. By the time you've replaced the place-holding text and graphics with your own – and then added whatever embellishments you feel are necessary – there's no reason why a publication based on a design should not look like anything other than entirely your own work.

Before you start

Treat the following step-by-step guide to creating business cards as a tutorial. It demonstrates many of the recurring techniques of using Publisher's designs so you should work through it even if you have no need for business cards at this time.

In order to complete the tutorial (or any of the business stationery projects) you'll need to create or acquire a company logo. An existing logo can be scanned in at a minimum of 150dpi, then cropped and saved as a TIFF file. A new logo can be created using Windows Paint or any image-editing program. Save the logo as Mylogo.tif.

An alternative approach is to create a WMF logo which can be scaled to any size without losing quality. If you already own CorelDRAW, Adobe Illustrator or any other drawing program, you can already export drawings in WMF format. If not, you can download a free graphics program, Zoner Draw 3, from **www.zoner.com**. Those who have no artistic inclinations can simply choose a piece of Office clip art and use that instead. Wherever your scalable logo comes from, call it Mylogo.wmf.

7w 3 is the only completely free version of the program available for download. Versions 4 and 5 are time-limited trial versions that must eventually be paid for.

Project 1 – Business cards

In this tutorial you'll make some business cards and, in the process, supply Publisher with personal information about yourself and a fictional company. This information will be reused in future projects. Completed business cards can be printed commercially or on your own printer using specially scored or perforated A4 card. When buying card it doesn't matter in what pattern the individual business cards are arranged on the sheet because you can customise the output options within Publisher to cope with any type of layout. If possible, the individual cards should be European standard size, which is 8.5cm x 5.5cm.

Start Publisher or, if the program is already running, click New on the File menu. In the New Publication task pane, click Design Sets, followed by Master Sets. In the Preview window, click Accent Box Business Card. This will cause the Personal Information dialogue box to be displayed. Complete the fields for name, job title, organization, address, phone, fax, e-mail and business motto. You will need to add a postcode to the address panel because the one we used is not visible in this screenshot. There is no need at this stage to decide whether to include a specific colour scheme, but if you later develop a preference for one of Publisher's schemes you can return to the Personal Information settings and select one. Do not click the Update button yet!

Up to four sets of personal information can be stored for different purposes. You have just completed the Primary Business set, which is the one Publisher uses by default. If you now open the drop-down box at the top of the dialogue box you'll see it is also possible to define sets for Secondary Business, Other Organization and Home/Family. Select Home/Family and fill in your own details. Before clicking Update, be sure to switch back to the Primary Business set of data. The Personal Information dialogue box will then close to reveal the business card. If you will be printing on cards other than 8.5cm x 5.5cm, open the File menu and click Page Setup. On the Layout tab change the Width and Height settings to match your cards. Click OK and then click Yes when Publisher offers to resize your cards.

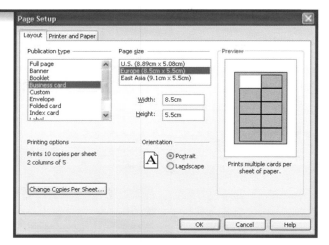

Most of the information on the card comes directly from the information provided in Step 1. The only exceptions to this are the graphic device in the top left corner and the company logo in the bottom right. The logo is in two parts, consisting of a small pyramid device and the word 'Organization'. The logo is not intended to be used in its present form, and there are two ways it can be changed: by replacing the pyramid with your own logo or by substituting your company's name for the word 'Organization', or by replacing both the text and the pyramid with a large version of your company logo. To try the first of these, click on the logo to select it, and then click a second time on the pyramid so that only the pyramid is selected.

4

With the pyramid selected, click the right mouse button to display a pop-up menu. Select *Change Picture* followed by *From File*. An Insert Picture dialogue box is then displayed, in which you should navigate to the folder where you stored Mylogo.tif or Mylogo.wmf. Select the appropriate file and click the Insert button. Your company logo replaces the pyramid, and you may then select the text beneath it and change it to the name of your company. You may also change the font and its colour by using the standard selection tools on the formatting toolbar or by opening the Format menu and clicking Font.

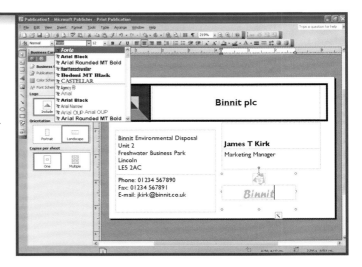

5

Save the publication as Bizcard1. After you have done so, you'll see a message box asking if you want to save the changes you have made to the logo. Click Yes. When you now open the Edit menu and select Personal Information, the dialogue box you used in Step 1 will reappear. You'll see that it now displays your company logo. This logo will be used by default in every future publication that requires one. There is no way to change this logo from within the Personal Information dialogue box. You must assign a new logo within a publication, and then save the publication in order to generate a message box asking if you also want to save the new logo.

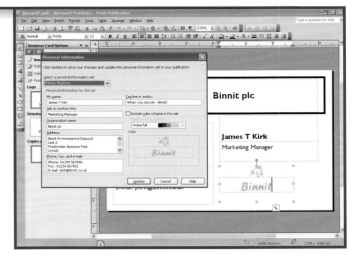

6

An alternative type of logo completely replaces the small logo and company name with a large logo. To see how this works, click the magic wand icon beneath the current logo. This displays a Logo Designs wizard in the task pane. Click Logo Options, followed by Inserted Picture. This activates the Choose picture button. Click the Choose picture button to produce the Insert Picture dialogue, where you can select your Mylogo file as you did in Step 4. If you like the new logo, save your publication as Bizcard 2 and click Yes to retain the logo. If you want to return to the two-part logo, click Publisher design in the task pane before saving the publication, and choose No when asked if you want to save the logo.

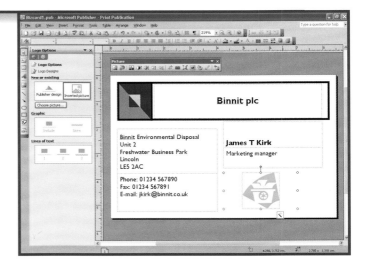

7

Whenever you use any design for the first time, it's worth clicking each of its elements in turn to see if there is a wizard associated with it. Only when an element is selected will its magic wand, if it has one, be displayed. On your business card there is a graphic design in the top left corner. When it is selected, you'll see a magic wand; by clicking the wand you can choose a different design from the five examples displayed in the task pane. In the screenshot, we've selected Bullseye.

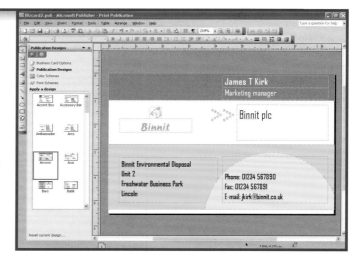

8

With Business Card Options displayed in the task pane (use the Back button at the top of the task pane to bring them into view if necessary) you'll see that two of the three required options are already correctly selected: Include Logo and Landscape. The third option is Copies per sheet, and this should be changed from One to Multiple because you'll be outputting your business cards onto a single sheet of A4 paper. You're now ready to experience the really impressive aspect of Publisher's design templates by clicking Publication Designs in the task pane. It's now possible to select any of the 53 plain-paper designs and see your business card change before your eyes. In addition, there are custom-made designs for pre-printed papers. These are only available from **www.paperdirect.co.uk** and cannot be displayed unless you install the special viewer for them when prompted. Every design, whether for plain or printed paper, has a unique name, so make a note of any that take your fancy for future use. When you've finished browsing, select the design called Arrows.

9

Having chosen a design, the next stage is to select a colour scheme. In the task pane, click Color Schemes, and then click through the list to see the effects. After browsing, select the scheme called Bluebird. In cases where you can't find a suitable colour scheme, you can click Custom color scheme at the bottom of the task pane to design your own in interactive mode. Custom colour schemes can be named and saved for future use.

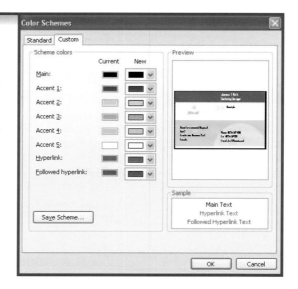

10

Finally, choose a suitable set of fonts by clicking Font Schemes in the task pane. The one used in this project is called Foundry. When experimenting with fonts, keep an eye on the address panel of your business card: you may find some font schemes cause you to lose the last line of your address. If this happens, simply select the offending text and change its point size until the missing text reappears. Notice in this example that, when the address panel is selected, there is a Text Overflow marker beneath it, indicating that the postcode has been pushed out of the panel. To fix this problem, change the point size of the text from 6.2 to 6. Whenever you change a default font scheme, you should make a note of the scheme's name and any adjustments to point sizes you feel are necessary. When all is well, save your publication as Bizcard3.

11

Even if you don't have any pre-scored paper to hand you can print your business cards on ordinary card or stiff paper and separate them using a guillotine. If you're using pre-scored paper you need to ascertain the vertical and horizontal gaps between labels, and determine the top and side margins. The paper we used for this project had top and side margins of 1.4cm, a horizontal gap of 1cm and no vertical gap between labels. When you've noted the measurements appropriate for your chosen paper, click Print Preview on the File menu and then click the Change Copies Per Sheet button.

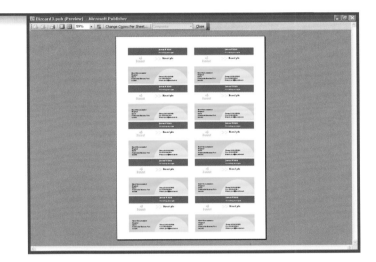

12

The Small Publication Print Options dialogue box is displayed. Enter the appropriate gap settings into its four input boxes and you'll see a diagrammatic representation on the right of the screen adjust itself automatically. Click OK when you've made the necessary changes, and then click Close. Save your publication again in order to make the revised print settings permanent. You can now print in the usual way, but if you'll be using coated or glossy paper don't forget to change the paper settings in your printer driver before printing. If you made notes regarding interesting designs, colour schemes and fonts, keep them in a safe place.

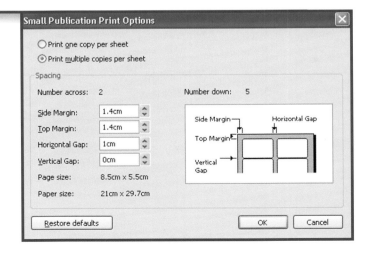

DTP PROJECTS

Business stationery

Large companies can afford to farm out design work to teams of experts whose mission is to bolster corporate identity as much as to produce stationery, while the owner of a small business is more likely to choose stationery designs from a sample book at a local print shop. Now, with the help of Microsoft Publisher's built-in design templates, businesses of any size can produce high-impact matching stationery with minimal effort.

Most businesses will have their stationery designs printed commercially because of the cost savings, but it is also possible to generate finished documents using a desktop printer. This might appeal to start-up businesses whose stationery requirements are still unclear, and to any business running short of stationery and in need of certain items to tide them over until a fresh batch can be ordered from a commercial printer.

A word of warning to anyone contemplating printing their own stationery: the ink in most inkjet printers is not permanent, and however impressive your stationery looks it will fail to do its job – and give out the wrong signals – if it smudges when handled. You can buy coated and glossy inkjet papers that won't smudge, but it might be better to print in black and white on a sub-£100 laser. It will certainly be cheaper, and you can always use textured or coloured papers for greater impact.

A desktop laser printer used in conjunction with coloured papers might be all you need to produce your own stationery in the quantities you need, when you need them.

Two approaches to stationery design

There are two ways of designing stationery in Microsoft Publisher: by using the built-in design templates or by starting from a blank page. In Project 2 you'll find out how to produce matching letterheads, envelopes and compliments slips with great ease, using simple modifications to existing templates.

Most business stationery follows predictable patterns so there is no reason not to use templates when they are available, but one example of a situation where templates can't do the job is when stationery is being designed for use with a proprietary accounts program that is only configured to print on purpose-designed paper. Project 3 demonstrates how to deal with this type of problem by showing you how to design a unique invoice, from scratch, for use with a specific accounts program; yet one which is still a perfect match for the template stationery produced in Project 2.

Microsoft Publisher includes special templates designed specifically for use with pre-printed papers from **www.paperdirect.co.uk**.

Project 2 – Letterheads, envelopes and compliments slips

To create a letterhead for Binnit plc, start Publisher or, if the program is already running, click New on the File menu. In the New Publication task pane, click Design Sets, followed by Master Sets. Select the Arrows set and then, in the Preview window, click Arrows Letterhead (you may have to scroll down to see it). If you've never made a letterhead, you'll be prompted to install the feature from the program CD. When the document is displayed on screen, zoom in to the address panel in the top right corner. To change any of the information shown here, click on the text to edit it. To change the information for all future documents, use the Personal Information option on the Edit menu.

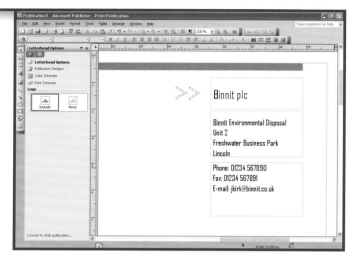

As this is a letterhead for a company rather than for an individual, the e-mail address of jkirk@binnit.co.uk should be removed, or replaced by a generic one such as postmaster@binnit.co.uk. To make the letterhead match the business card produced in Project 1, click on Color Schemes and select Bluebird, and then click on Font Schemes and select Foundry. The only optional design element is the logo, which is displayed by default above the coloured bar at the bottom of the page. It can be turned on or off after clicking Letterhead Options by using the Include and None icons, or you can reposition the logo by dragging it.

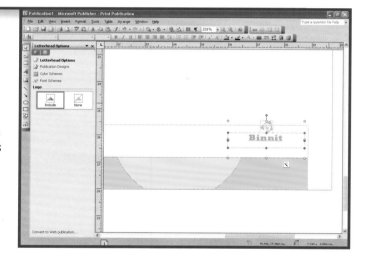

Before creating a matching envelope, save the letterhead, then click New on the File menu. In the New Publication task pane, click Design Sets, followed by Master Sets. Select the Arrows set and then, in the Preview window, click Arrows Envelope. If you've never made an envelope, you'll be prompted to install the feature from the program CD. Under Envelope options in the task pane you can choose whether or not to print the logo, and you may choose an envelope size of C6 or DL (the example uses DL). These are standard sizes for business communications and are suitable for folded A4 paper. If you wish to create any other size of envelope, open the File menu and click Page Setup. On the Layout tab, select Envelope as the Publication type and then use the Page size panel to choose another standard envelope size or define a custom one.

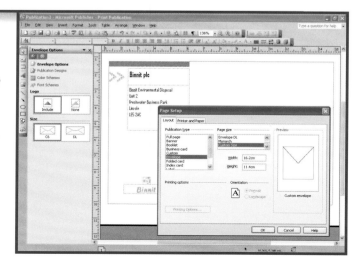

4

Under Color Schemes, select Bluebird and, under Font Schemes, select Foundry. These are selected in accordance with the business cards and letterheads already produced. Because the Foundry font scheme uses larger fonts than the originals, the text box containing the address lines is not tall enough. Confirm this by clicking on the address panel and you'll see a Text Overflow icon. To fix the problem, click on the text box and enlarge it vertically. Save a copy of the publication as EnvAddress, and then select the address text box and delete it. Save another copy of the envelope as EnvBlank. In future, you'll load EnvAddress when you want to type in a unique address and print a single envelope and you'll load EnvBlank if you want to print a stack of blank envelopes suitable for mail merging or manual typing.

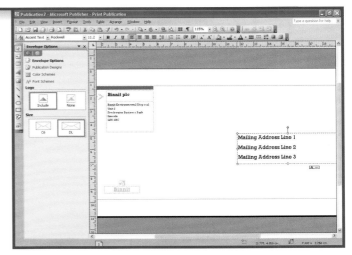

5

To create a compliments slip, start a new publication as before. Unfortunately there is no template for a compliments slip in the Arrows Design Set (not all publication types are available in every set) so use the Bars Design Set instead. Select Bars with Compliments Card. If you've never made a compliments slip, you'll be prompted to install the feature from the program CD. As soon as the compliments slip is displayed, use the Color Schemes option to select Bluebird and the Font Schemes option to select Foundry.

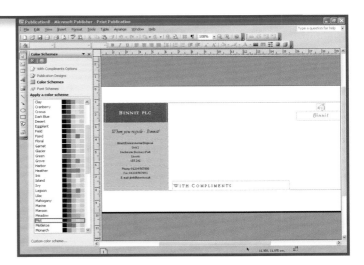

6

As you did with the letterhead, you might wish to edit the contact information on the slip to make it more generic by changing the e-mail address. In the task pane, click With Compliments Options, and then use the controls there to determine whether or not to print the logo, and whether to print single or multiple copies per sheet. The Multiple option prints three slips on A4; the One option centres a single label per A4 sheet. The latter saves ink or toner but requires just as much effort to trim. Save your compliments slip and then close the three publications you've created during this project.

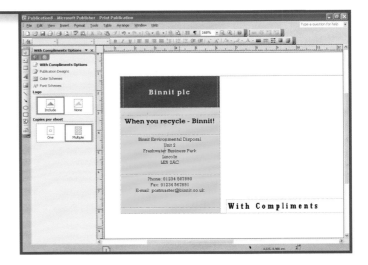

Project 3 – A purpose-designed invoice

Many businesses use off-the-shelf computer programs that demand special paper when printing items such as sales receipts, packing lists, shipping labels and invoices. In order to create your own pre-printed forms for use with these programs you need to duplicate the layout of the official stationery. It's unusual for the vendors of such programs to provide a detailed specification of the required paper layout (after all, they want to sell you their own paper!) but armed with a ruler and a few sheets of sample output from the program, you can create your own paper and tailor it to match the rest of your company's stationery.

This project is based on the output from an invoicing program. It shows customer number, order number, invoice number, invoice date and customer's address. Below these are five columns in which items sold can be listed, and beneath these are the usual totals for VAT, carriage etc. It is necessary to measure where each field of information begins, relative to the top of the page and the left-hand edge. You also need to know how much space to allocate for the longest possible entry in each field. For the sake of the exercise, you'll be provided with this information as you proceed through the steps.

In order to create a form that matches the output of a computer program you'll need some sample output on blank or pre-printed paper, like this invoice from an accounts package.

```
      SG1237547


Caroline Carpenter                         1407864
Fulton House
123 Boroughbridge Lane                     1243234
Harrogate
Yorkshire                                  05/03/2006
YO5 678



102345       Sharps disposal drum        1    10.34    10.34
114534       Heavy duty latex gloves     3     7.95    23.85
```

```
                                                   34.19

                                                    8.00

                                                    0.00

                                                    7.38

                                                   49.57
```

1

While it would be possible to start with a completely blank page and add a corporate identity afterwards, you can save time by starting with the letterhead you saved in the previous project. Load the letterhead into Publisher, and then click to select the address panel. Drag it off the document and store it at the side of the document in the grey work area. Repeat this procedure with the contact panel and the logo at the bottom of the page. You'll use them later.

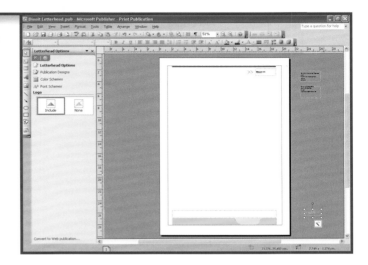

2

Most of the invoice will be taken up by a table, but there will also be five text boxes at the top. To make it easy to position them correctly, you'll create ruler guides at positions determined by measuring the blank invoice. Click anywhere on the publication and then zoom to 100% (don't forget the F9 shortcut), open the Arrange menu and click Snap. Make sure that To Ruler Marks and To Guides are selected.

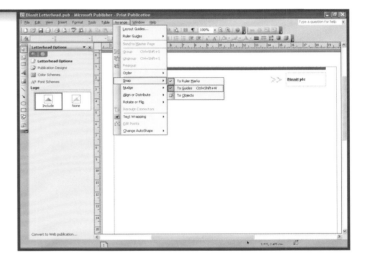

3

Drag out a guide from the top ruler and position it at 37mm. This is for the top of the Customer ID number. Drag out another for the bottom of the ID number at 42mm. For the address, you'll need guides at 52mm and 74mm. For the top of the main table you need a guide at 85mm, and for the start of the table itself another at 94mm. Nearer the bottom of the page are five figures showing charges. You'll need to scroll down the page and position the guides for these at 206mm, 212mm, 219mm, 226mm, 233mm and 239mm.

④

Now pull out vertical guides from the left-hand ruler and position them at 31mm, 55mm, 85mm, 116mm, 125mm, 144mm and 171mm. Don't forget that if you have trouble placing guides manually you can set them (in centimetres) using the Ruler Guides dialogue box. This is opened from the Arrange menu by clicking Ruler Guides, then Format Ruler Guides.

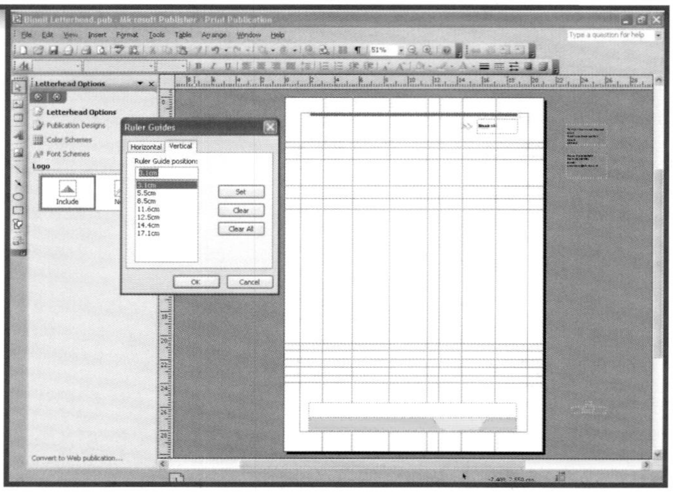

⑤

Zoom in on the top left corner of the publication. Click on the Text box icon in the left-hand toolbar and draw out a text box between the first two horizontal guides and the first three vertical ones. Type Customer ID. Because you're using the Foundry font scheme saved with the Binnit letterhead, this will be in Rockwell at 9.2 points. Place a border around the text box: click the right mouse button and select Format Text Box; on the Colors and Lines tab of the Format Text dialogue box, ensure that Color is set to black and Weight is set to 0.75pt. To force the same formatting on future text boxes, tick the box at the bottom labelled Apply settings to new text boxes. Click OK to finish.

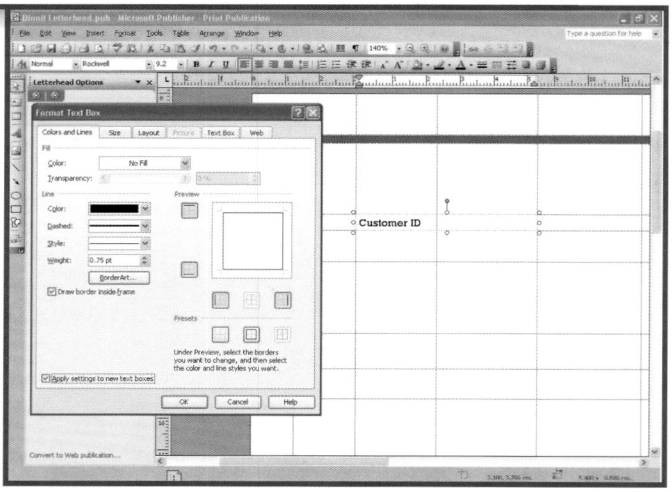

⑥

In a similar way create a text box for the address. Place it below the Customer ID as shown here. Create three more text boxes on the right-hand side of the page. They are 5mm in height, spaced 2mm apart, and they extend from the 116mm guide to the 171mm guide. The easiest way of creating them is to drag and position the top box, then press Ctrl+C to copy it. Paste two copies of the box by pressing Ctrl+V twice, then drag the copies into position. Into each cell enter the text labels shown here.

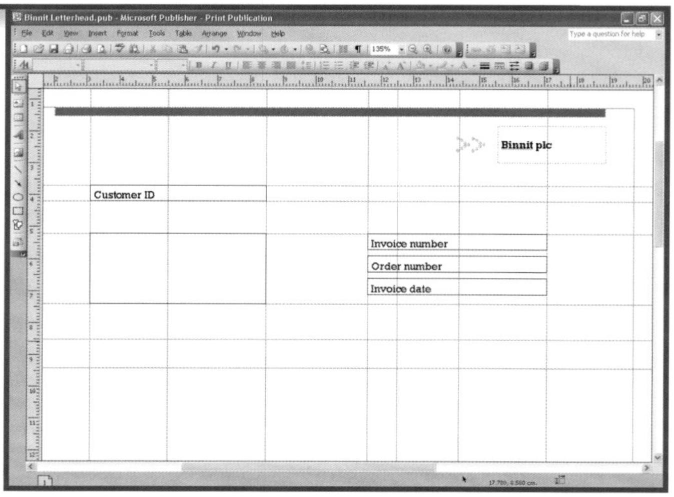

7

The main table is best inserted using Whole Page view. Click on the Insert Table icon on the left-hand toolbar (or use Insert, Table on the Table menu) and then drag out a table as shown here. Its top left corner is the intersection between the 85mm horizontal and 31mm vertical guides. Its bottom right corner is the intersection between the 239mm horizontal and 171mm vertical guides. When the Create Table dialogue box appears, change the number of rows to 7 and the number of columns to 5, then click OK.

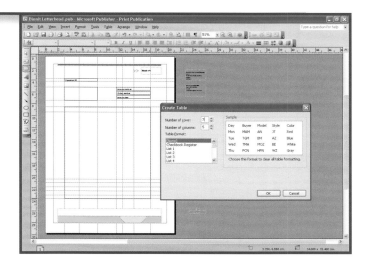

8

You now need to adjust the horizontal and vertical lines of the table so that they align with the ruler guides you placed earlier. Note that the 85mm vertical guide is not used. When you position the table dividing lines, start at the top and work down, and then work from left to right. Getting these lines into position is harder than it sounds because it's too easy to grab the ruler guides by mistake, so you should save the publication as TempInvoice before making adjustments to the table. If things go wrong and the Undo command can't fix them, you can reload the document and start this step again.

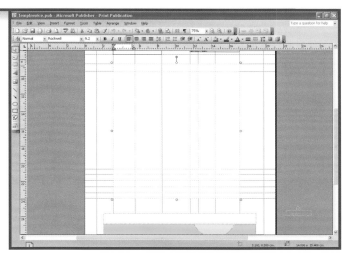

9

Hold down the left mouse button and drag to select the first two rows of the table. Right-click and select Format Table. In the Line section of the Format Table dialogue box, change Color to Black and click the rightmost of the three Presets icons. This will select all vertical and horizontal lines for bordering, and will set the line weight at 1pt. Use the Weight control to change this to 0.75pt, which is the same weight you used for the text box borders. Click OK, and then click anywhere off the table to see the effect.

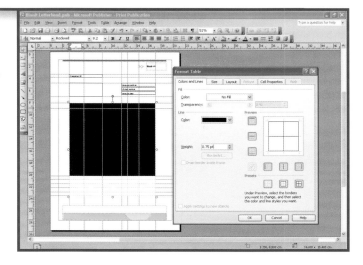

10

Using the same procedures as in the previous step, draw borders around the ten cells in the bottom right corner of the table, and then type the labels shown here. Drag the logo and the two text boxes from the grey work area onto the bottom of the invoice. Position and size them appropriately. Add a VAT registration number after the e-mail address.

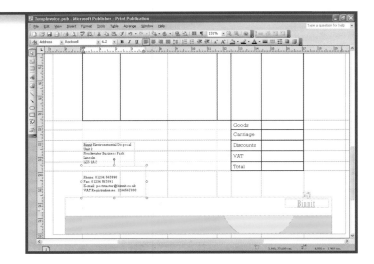

11

In the top row of the table, type the labels Item, Description, Qty, Unit Price and Total Price. Select all five labels by dragging, and then use the controls on the formatting toolbar to centre the labels and embolden them. Click the Fill Color icon and change it to black, and click the Font Color icon and change it to white. Click off the table to see the effect. All that remains is to draw a text box at the top and insert the word INVOICE. Increase the font size to 14 and embolden the text.

12

In a real situation rather than an exercise, you'd now save your invoice and test the layout by printing a few examples and running some sample data through your accounts program. As you can't do this, we've done it for you. You'll notice that the Customer ID is slightly out of kilter, and the text labels for some items don't exactly line up with the corresponding data. These defects can be fixed quite easily by adjusting the dividing lines of the table or altering the formatting of the text labels, but for non-perfectionists this invoice is probably good enough already.

PART 3

Marketing and promotional materials

Business stationery plays an important part in corporate branding. Customers soon learn to associate the fonts, graphics and colour combinations used on stationery with a specific company, so stationery designs tend not to be changed very often, if at all. In contrast, businesses also need to generate material such as flyers and promotional leaflets that do change frequently, either because their primary aim is to be novel and grab potential customers' attention or, in the case of brochures, catalogues and price lists, because their contents need to be kept up to date.

For the small business operator who has to design and produce promotional material as well as run a business from day to day, it's important to be able to produce sales and marketing material cheaply and effectively, which is why Publisher's design templates are so useful. In Project 4 you'll practise the basic techniques that enable any type of promotional material to be quickly generated, while in Project 5 you'll concentrate on a single item – a price list brochure – and see it not only through the design process but also use it in conjunction with a customer data file to create price lists printed with personalised addresses suitable for distribution in window envelopes.

Project 4 – Basic techniques for promotional publications

The techniques you'll use to create this special offer flyer can be applied to other promotional materials such as brochures, catalogues, informational postcards and ordinary flyers. As with most business documents in Microsoft Publisher, your first port of call after starting a new document is the Design Sets/Master Sets section. Click to select the Axis design set and then browse the Preview window for flyers. There are two: one for informational flyers and another for special offers. Click Axis Special Offer Flyer.

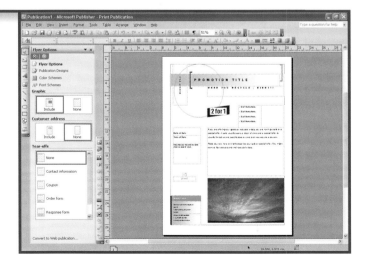

By default, the Primary Business details for Binnit are inserted into the publication. For this and future projects we'll abandon the Binnit theme, so click the Personal Information option on the Edit menu. When the Personal Information dialogue box is displayed, open the drop-down panel at the top and select Secondary Business. Enter the details shown here (adding a postcode to the address section). When you click the Update button, the new company's details will be inserted into the publication.

Personal Information

Click Update to save your changes and update this personal information set in your publication.

Select a personal information set:

Secondary Business

Personal information for this set

My name:

Peter Prentiss

Job or position title:

Proprietor

Organization name:

Classix Accessories

Address:

Classix Accessories
55 Holly Lane
Bracknell
Berks

Phone, fax, and e-mail:

Phone: 01234 567890
Fax: 01234 567891
E-mail: pp@coolclassix.co.uk

Tag line or motto:

Cool accessories for all classic cars

☐ Include color scheme in this set

Select a color scheme:

Tuscany

Logo

[Update]   [Cancel]   [Help]

Select and delete the Binnit logo – or change the logo to something more appropriate using the procedures described in Project 1. Zoom in to 100 per cent on the top half of the page. The text boxes you can see are of two types, according to whether they contain editable or replaceable text. Those with editable text are the ones displaying data taken from the Personal Information dialogue box. You can click on this text and edit it in the normal way. The replaceable text boxes contain instructions on how you should use the box, such as 'Promotion Title' and 'List items here'. It's easy to tell which type of box is which: when you click on editable text you see an editing cursor within the text, but when you click on replaceable text the entire text is selected and shaded black. Click on the 'List items here' box to see how this works.

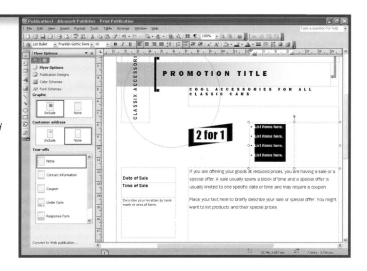

④

With the 'List items here' box selected, type in up to six key points. If you type more than four they'll overflow into the box on the right. When this has been done, insert suitable advertising copy into all the other replacement text boxes. The 2 for 1 graphic is actually a special kind of text box. If you click on it you'll see a magic wand icon appear beneath it. Click the wand and 36 designs will appear in the task pane on the left. Click to select one of these, and then click on the associated text and replace it with words of your own. Feel free to adjust the sizes of any of the text boxes if your own text is longer or shorter.

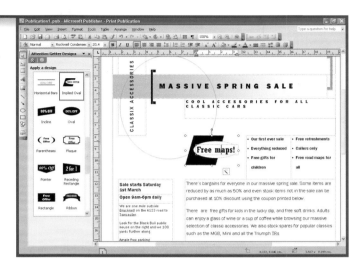

⑤

Switch to Whole Page view and click on the picture. This selects the picture frame. To select the picture itself, click again. You can now replace the picture with one of your own choosing by right-clicking to produce a context menu and then selecting Change Picture. If you don't see a Change Picture option, it's because you've only clicked once on the picture. You must click twice. The replacement can be a piece of clip art or another photograph. If it's a photograph you can select it from a file saved on your hard disk or download it immediately from a scanner or digital camera. The clip art or graphic will resize itself to fit the frame. If you insert clip art there'll be a Clip art search tool open in the task pane and you'll have to click the back arrow in the task pane to return to Flyer Options.

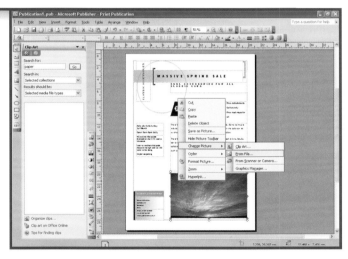

⑥

The Flyer Options in the task pane allow you to exclude the graphic if you'd rather have more space for text. There's also the option to include a customer address. If you choose to do this, an address panel is printed on the back of the flyer in a position that will make it visible when using window envelopes. How you might take advantage of this facility to print personalised names and addresses from a customer database is covered in Project 5. Also in Flyer Options is the ability to include one of five different tear-offs (a tear-off being anything the customer cuts out, such as an order form or a coupon). Click the Coupon option to insert one in your flyer.

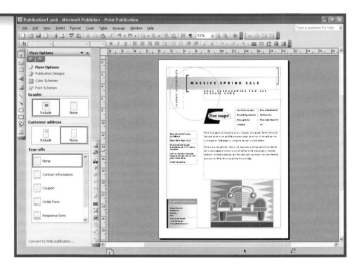

7

The picture and certain other page elements are automatically rearranged to make way for the coupon at the bottom. Zoom in and click on the coupon to produce a magic wand icon beneath it. Click the wand icon and the task pane changes to show three different coupon designs. Select Top Oval, then click Coupon Options. Select the More Text and Cutout Dashes options, and then click on the various text elements in the coupon and insert replacement text that makes sense for your flyer.

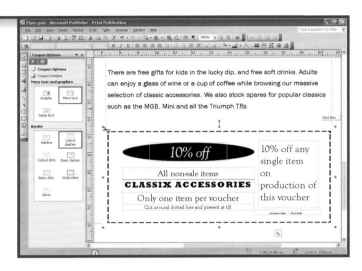

8

Your flyer is almost complete. All that remains is to adjust the position or size of any frame that looks out of place. In this screenshot, we've increased the size of the coupon and moved it into line with the other frames. Now for the fun part! (First save your document as Flyer.pub.) Use the options in the task pane to experiment with different designs, colours and font schemes. Some of them will adversely affect the layout, which is why you saved the publication first, but there's always a chance you'll find something you like better than the existing design. If you do change the style of the publication, you must also be prepared to make minor adjustments to frame sizes and fonts.

Project 5 – A mail-merged price list

In this project, you'll create a data file of names and addresses using a spreadsheet program; then in Publisher you'll create a three-panel folded price list with an address panel on the back; finally you'll merge the data file with the price list and print off some addressed copies. Publisher can accept data in many forms – from spreadsheets, databases, or directly from an Outlook contacts folder – but you'll use the CSV (comma-separated values) format because it can be produced by any spreadsheet or word processor.

Set up your data file like the one shown here, with labels in row 1 and addresses on the four rows beneath, then save it as Customers.csv *using the Save As function of your spreadsheet. In the unlikely event that a spreadsheet program is not available, you can create a CSV file in a word processor by typing the labels on the first line and the addresses (one per line) beneath. Where there would be a cell-dividing line in a spreadsheet, use a comma instead. Where there would be a blank cell in a spreadsheet, insert an extra comma. Save the addresses in plain text format as* Customers.csv.

Start Publisher and create a new document. In the task pane, click Design Sets, Master Sets, Blends. In the Preview window, select Blends Price List Brochure. Use the Personal Information option on the Edit menu to switch to the Secondary Business data (for Classix Accessories). Select and delete the Binnit logo. Click on the Page 2 icon at the bottom of the screen to view the other side of the brochure.

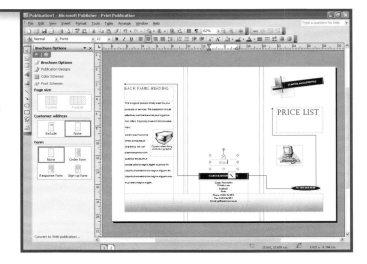

❸

It's on this page that in a real-world situation you would enter details of your company in the first panel, and the prices of individual items in panels two and three. To replace the prices in panel three with an order form, click Order Form in the task pane on the left. If you want to experiment further with this side of the brochure, do so now, but no further editing is required for the completion of the project. When you're ready, click on the Page 1 icon to return to the other side of the brochure.

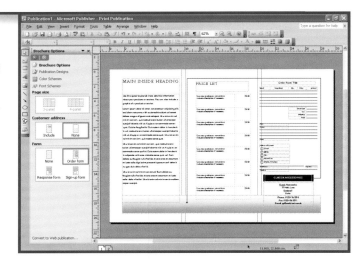

❹

In the task pane, in the Customer Address section, click Include. This will insert an envelope design in the middle panel. If you use standard DL window envelopes, the address panel should match up fine with its window. For non-standard window envelopes, print and fold a copy of the brochure and try it in one of your own envelopes. Make whatever adjustments are necessary by dragging the address text box into a different position.

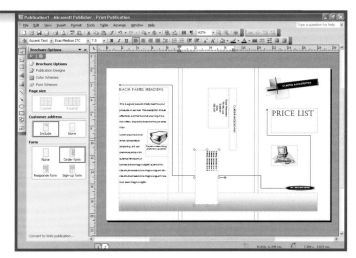

❺

Zoom in on the address panel, select the replaceable address lines and delete them. On the Tools menu, select Mail and Catalog merge, followed by Mail and Catalog merge wizard. The wizard is controlled via the task pane, where Mail Merge is already selected. At the bottom of the task pane, click Next to continue. In the task pane, click Browse. When the Select Data Source dialogue box appears, navigate to Customers.csv and click Open. A small dialogue box with a long title appears: Text File Connection Parameters. Select Comma as the separator, and tick the box to confirm that the first row of data contains column headers. Click OK.

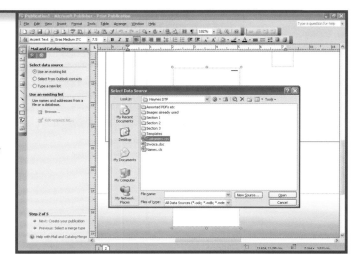

6

In the Mail Merge Recipients dialogue box, you can sort the customer list in various ways, select a specific set of customers using the Find command, or choose individual addresses using the tick boxes on the left. Experiment with these if you wish, but for the purposes of this project all you need do is to click OK to work with all four addresses. Having done this, click Next at the bottom of the task pane.

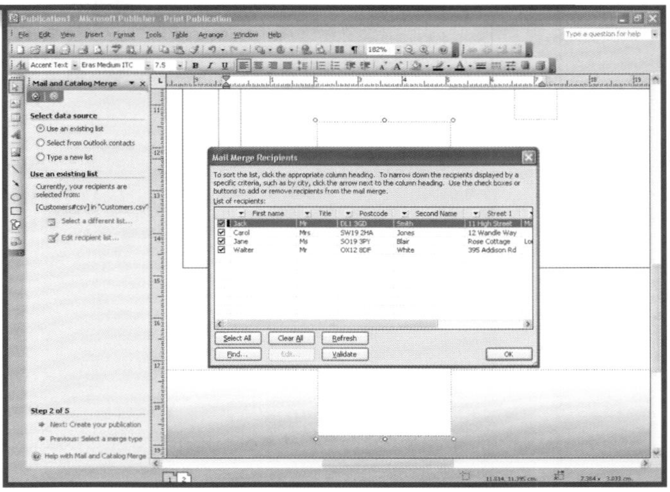

7

In the task pane, click Address Block. When the Insert Address Block dialogue box appears, click Match Fields. In the Match Fields dialogue box, use the drop-down lists on the right to tell Publisher which of its field names match the field names used in your data file. Some of them are guessed correctly by Publisher. The ones you need to match for yourself are Last Name to Second Name; Address 1 to Street 1; City to Town; State to County; Address 2 to Street 2. Click OK when you've made the selections, then click OK to close the Insert Address Block dialogue box.

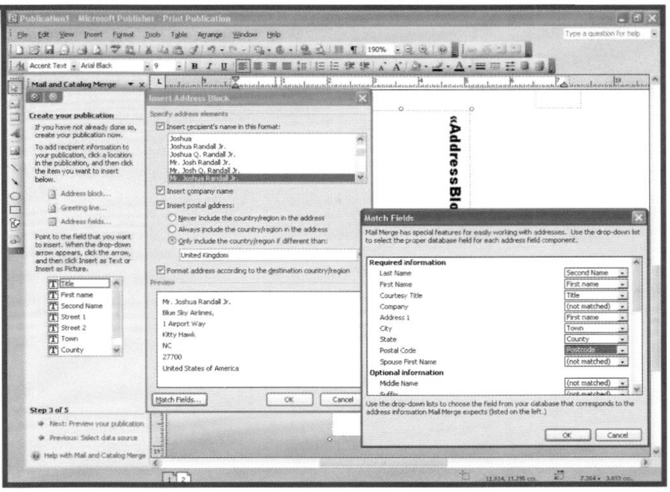

8

Click Next at the bottom of the task pane and the first address will be displayed. The buttons at the top of the task pane can be used to scroll back and forth between the addresses, and individual customers can be dropped from the list by clicking the Exclude this recipient button. If you don't like the formatting of the addresses you can select the address text and change it to a clearer font or larger point size. Click Next to continue, then click the Print option in the task pane. In the Print dialogue box, use the Test button to print just one price list as a test. Save the completed publication.

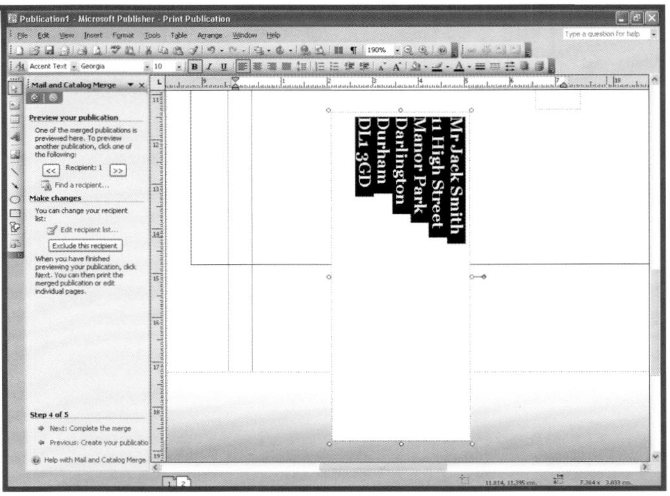

PART **3** Home and personal projects

It would be unproductive for business users to spend their time creating personalised greetings cards and picture postcards, or assembling wall posters from taped-together sheets of A4 paper, but for home users these activities can be both enjoyable and productive. The creator of a personalised publication gets a kick out of making it, and the recipient gets an equal kick out of the compliment it pays him or her. There's no reason why desktop publishing shouldn't be fun – and don't forget that personalised publications make great gifts if they're printed with care on good-quality media.

Project 6 – Greetings cards and invitations

There are hundreds of greetings card designs in Publisher 2003 for all sorts of occasions and anniversaries. They come with appropriate graphics, greetings, jokes and verses, all of which can be adapted by you to create a truly personal card. A greetings card has a front, back and two inside pages, which are displayed separately as pages one to four in Publisher. When you print the card, all four pages are printed onto the same side of A4 paper or card, with Publisher taking care of the positioning and rotation of the pages so that they're all in the right places when folded.

Invitation cards are virtually identical to greetings cards in terms of how you define and print them, but there are fewer designs to choose from and some of the customisation options are restricted. You can apply the same procedures described in this project to invitations and other folded publications.

1

Start Publisher, or select New on the File menu if it is already running. Click Publications for Print in the task pane. Click Greetings Cards. In the list of special occasions click Get Well, and then, in the Preview window, select Get Well Card 2.

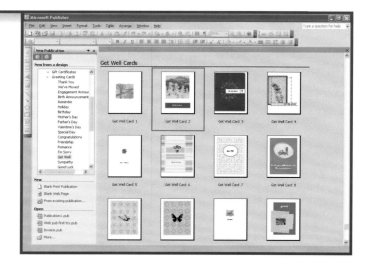

2

In the Design section of the task pane, you can see that the current design is called Greetings Bar. Clicking on any of the other designs will change the card completely; not only its cover but also the inside and back pages. The changes are reflected almost instantly in the main window.

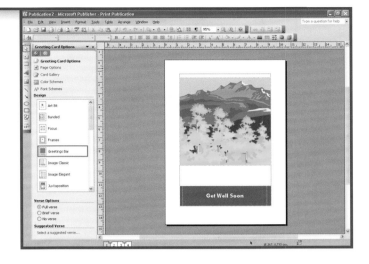

3

This is the Juxtaposition design, which by default uses the Tropics colour scheme and Wizard font scheme. By changing the display colours and fonts you can greatly alter the appearance of the card, making it look more or less formal as required.

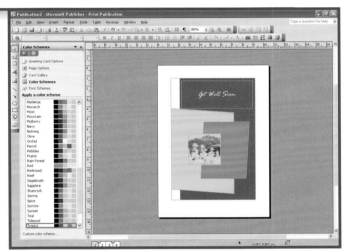

4

The Ivy colour scheme and Casual font set have been selected. Before making any further changes you should determine in which orientation it will be printed. Click Page Options in the task pane and choose one of the three options: side-fold, top-fold or half-page.

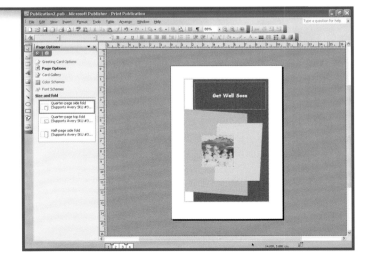

5

To use a personalised picture, right-click on the mountain scene and select Change Picture. You can then choose a piece of clip art or a photograph or graphic stored on your hard disk. You may even scan an image directly into the publication.

6

To view the message inside the card (Publisher calls it a verse), click the Page 2 or Page 3 icon at the bottom of the screen. The message is contained in two separate text boxes, and this one is rather formal. You can change it by clicking in each box in turn and typing your own message, including the name of the recipient, or you can select Greeting Card Options in the task pane and then click 'Select a suggested verse' at the bottom.

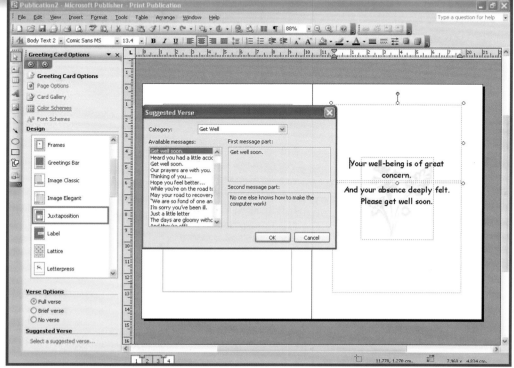

Click on the Page 4 icon and you'll see a message on the back saying 'Made especially for you by:' and then a name taken from the Personal Information Primary Business set. If the name shown is not yours, you can click on it and change it, or you can click Personal Information on the Edit menu and change from the Primary Business set to Home/Family, where your name is stored.

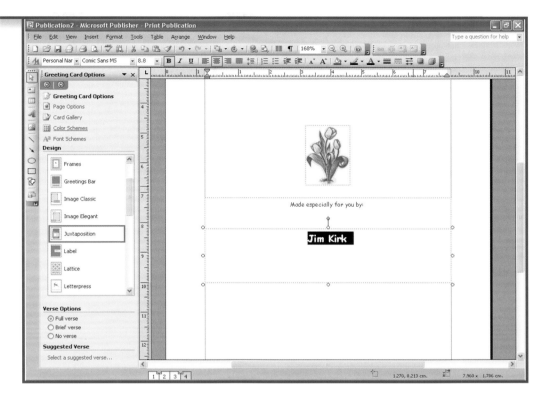

Save the card for future use, and then click Print Preview on the File menu to check that all is well. For best results load a paper of 120gsm or heavier into your printer, and don't forget to set the correct option in your printer driver if the paper is coated or glossy.

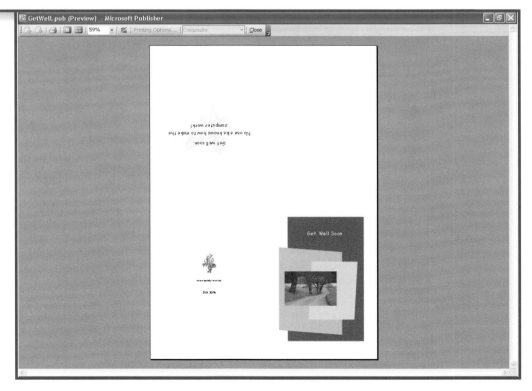

Project 7 – Posters and banners

Banners are to posters as invitations are to greetings cards. In other words, a banner is just a simplified poster. It is made up of pages joined horizontally to other pages to create a wide publication, whereas a poster can be attached to other pages on all sides to create a large rectangular publication. Printing your own posters or banners is too time-consuming to do on a regular basis, but for parties, celebrations and special occasions, it can be great fun.

Joining pages together to create large publications would be fraught with difficulties if you had to plan for all the printing peculiarities yourself, but Publisher simplifies the entire process by building in an overlap where pages join, and providing crop and alignment marks for trimming and joining. Once you've tackled a poster you'll have no problems with banners.

1

Start Publisher, or select New on the File menu if it is already running. Click Blank Publications in the task pane, and then select Poster in the main Preview window. Unless you're aiming for something very stark and dramatic you'll want a border or background for your poster. This one is called Bubbles.

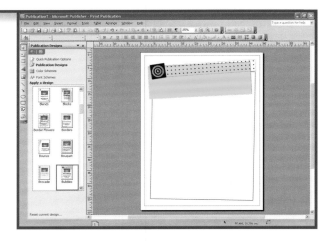

2

Although you can add text boxes and picture frames to your poster wherever you like, it's easier to start with a ready-made framework. Click Quick Publication Options in the task pane and choose one of the layouts on display. They're not named: this is the leftmost one in row three.

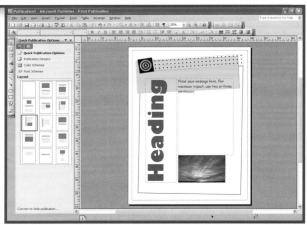

3

Enter the text for your poster. The body text in this example has been enlarged and emboldened. To change the picture, right-click on it and select Change Picture. You can then choose to insert a piece of clip art, a picture stored on your hard disk, or to scan directly into the publication.

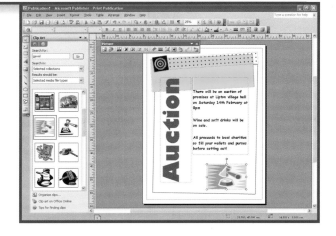

4

The additional text was created by copying the Auctions text frame, then dragging one of its corner handles to resize it. The text was then rotated to a suitable angle using the green handle and finally dragged into position.

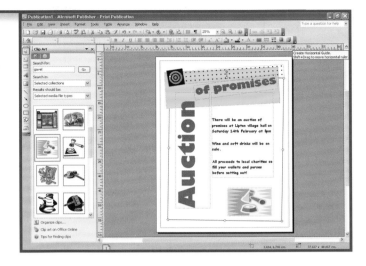

5

When you're happy with the poster, save it, and then choose Page Setup on the file menu. The diagram in the dialogue box makes it clear how many sheets of paper are required for a 45cm x 60cm poster. You may change the size to 60cm x 90cm, or type your own figures into the Width and Height boxes. When you're done, click OK to close the dialogue box and then print the poster.

6

The sheets are printed with a 0.635cm overlap on the right and bottom edges, which is where you apply the glue. The top and left edges should be cut to the trim marks. Assemble and glue the top row of sheets from left to right, and then assemble each of the other rows in turn. It's easier if you glue them to a larger backing surface.

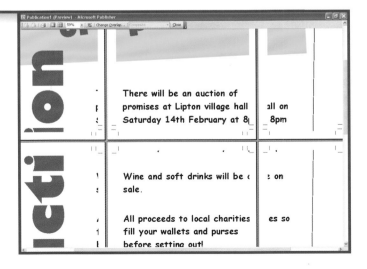

Project 8 – Calendars and single-sided publications

Single-sided publications are items such as calendars, award certificates, gift certificates, letterheads and printed postcards. All of them can be generated effortlessly using Publisher's built-in design templates, but a certain amount of customisation is always necessary, even if it's only to specify a date or venue. If you want to go further, you can, with your own choice of colours, fonts, graphical embellishments and photographs. In this project, we use a calendar as the archetypal single-sided publication. A calendar is no harder or easier to produce than any of the other single-sided publications, but it's a good one to start with because it makes an acceptable gift and it's an excellent way of displaying digital photographs.

1

Start Publisher, or select New on the File menu if it is already running. Click Publications for Print in the task pane. Click Calendars, then Full Page (if you have never made a calendar, you will be prompted to insert the program CD). There are several designs suitable for displaying photographs. This one is Photo Album. The others are Art Left, Art Right, Pinstripes, Travel and Varsity.

2

Photo Album works well whatever the shape of your picture, and it looks good in both landscape and portrait orientations. In the task pane, choose Portrait, then click the Font Schemes option to choose one you like. This one is called Monogram.

3

Click on Calendar Options. Leave the 'Month or year' option set to Monthly, then click the 'Change date range' button. In order to produce a set of 12 calendars for 2007, set Start date to January 2007 and End date to December 2007. Click OK. If you want to produce a calendar for a single month, just set the Start and End dates to the same month.

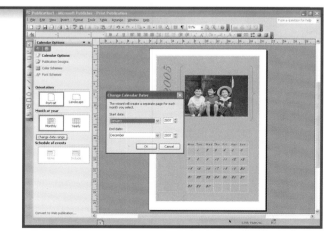

4

When the calendars have been generated, you'll see row of 12 page icons at the bottom of the screen, with Page 12 selected. Click on the icon for Page 1. Right-click on the picture and select Change Picture. Click 'From File', if the picture is already on your hard disk, or 'From Scanner or Camera', if it isn't.

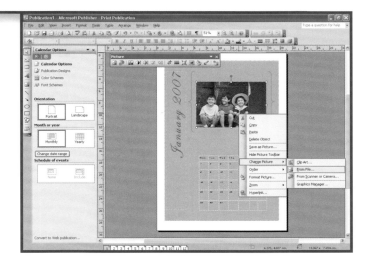

5

When you've inserted the picture, resize it if necessary by dragging one of its corners while holding down a Shift key to constrain the picture to its original proportions. Reposition it if necessary. Click the Color Schemes option in the task pane and choose a scheme that provides a suitable mix of font and background colours for the photo. This one is Eggplant.

6

Click on each of the remaining page icons in turn, repeating Steps 3 and 4 to insert a new picture and pick new colours for each month. You may also click on any individual day in a calendar and add notes or reminders. When you've finished, save the entire publication prior to printing. The default option is to print all 12 calendars, so for test purposes you may wish to choose Current page only.

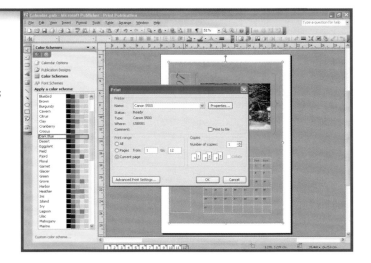

Project 9 – Newsletters and multi-page publications

Multi-page publications such as newsletters, catalogues and books are the hardest to automate, and newsletters are the hardest of all. Publisher 2003 will happily create a newsletter for you, but the chances of your stories and pictures matching the sizes and shapes of the frames provided are virtually non-existent. More awkward still, the automated Newsletter template does not use a master page layout, so if you try to modify the layouts provided for you, there are no guides or columns to help.

In this project, we sidestep these difficulties by showing you how to design a newsletter from scratch using a master page layout. Although the newsletter is for a fictitious community group, we've kept the style formal so that it can also be used for commercial purposes.

If you've already followed the step-by-step instructions in the first part of Section 2, you'll have a suitable template called A4grid3x6 in your Publisher Templates folder. If not, you'll need to create the template before tackling this project. You'll also need some *lorem ipsum* text that you can copy and paste, plus a head-and-shoulders photograph, and a clip art picture of a stylised eye. We downloaded our eye picture from the web by searching for 'all-seeing' in the Publisher Clip art task pane.

① *Start Publisher, or select New on the File menu if it is already running. Click Templates in the task pane and select A4grid3x6 from the Preview window. Unless you've saved more templates of your own, it will be the only one there. Open the Arrange menu and use the Snap option to ensure that snapping is set to guides and ruler marks, but not to objects. Open the Edit menu and click Personal Information. Select the Other Organisation personal information set and type the data shown here. Click Update.*

② *To create a masthead, click Design Gallery Object on the left-hand toolbar (also available via the Insert menu). In the Design Gallery, with the Mastheads category selected, scroll downwards and select Voyage Masthead, then click Insert Object. Position the masthead as shown here, by dragging its corners until they snap to the master page grid. Change 'Newsletter Title' to 'The Local Eye' and 'Newsletter Date' to the actual publication date.*

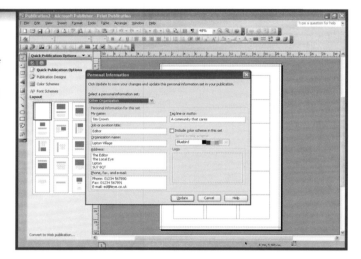

To change the compass graphic on the masthead to a more appropriate all-seeing eye, click first on the compass to select the entire masthead, and then again on the compass to select the graphic itself. When the compass is selected, right-click and select Change Picture, followed by From File. Navigate to where you stored the all-seeing eye graphic on your hard disk, then click Insert. Now pull down a guide from the top ruler to the 8.5cm mark on the vertical ruler. This will serve as a positioning guide for the main story headline.

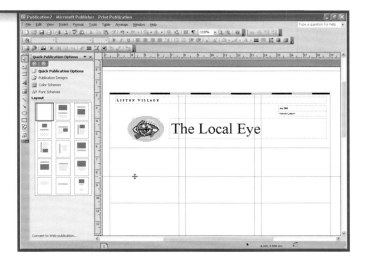

Click the Text Box icon in the side toolbar and then drag out a text box that spans the first two columns and stretches from the masthead to the 8.5cm ruler guide. Type the headline 'Lipton girl wins scholarship to famous stage school', then select the headline and use the formatting toolbar to set its font to Arial, bold, 20 points.

Right-click on the headline and select Format Text Box. On the Colors and Lines tab, click the leftmost Presets button to clear any existing selections, and then click the button for a bottom line. Change Color from No Line to black, and set Weight to 1pt. Now click on the Text Box tab and change Vertical Alignment to Bottom. Click OK. If this has the effect of pushing the headline text upwards, select the headline text box, open the Arrange menu, select order and click Bring to Front.

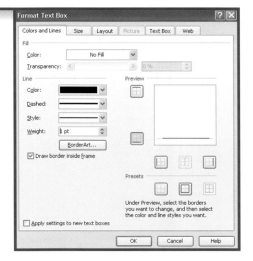

6

Create one text box in each column, reaching from the 8.5cm ruler guide to the horizontal guide two-thirds of the way down the page. Click in the first text box to select it, then paste in six or more paragraphs of lorem ipsum text. When you are asked if you want to use autoflow, click No. On the Tools menu, click Spelling, Hide Spelling Errors to clean up the display.

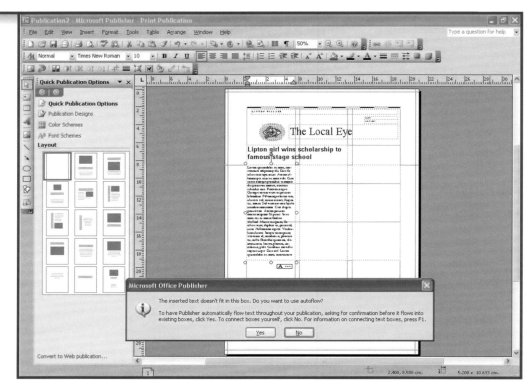

7

With the first text box selected, click on the Create Text Box Link icon on the Connect Text Boxes toolbar (seen here dragged onto the main screen). When the cursor changes to a pouring jug, click on the second text box to fill it with the overflow text. Repeat this process to pour text into the third column. Don't worry if it overflows.

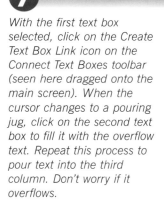

8

Click on the first text box and press Ctrl+A to select the text in all three boxes. On the Format menu, click Paragraph. In the Paragraph dialogue box, set Indentation Preset to 1st Line Indent, and First Line to 0.5cm. Change Line spacing After paragraphs from blank to 0pt. Click OK. With the text in all three boxes still selected, use the formatting toolbar to change the font to Times New Roman, 9 points.

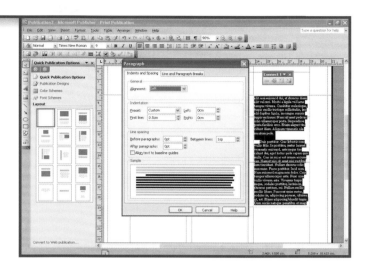

9

It is customary to include a table of contents on the first page of a newsletter to show what's on the other pages. To add one of these, open the Design Gallery and in the Tables of Contents category select Summer Table of Contents and click Insert Object. Position the table at the bottom of the first column, using the grid lines for guidance.

10

Pull down a ruler guide from the top ruler to the 21cm mark. Use this guide to create two text boxes reaching down to the bottom of the second and third columns, as shown here. Then create a third text box spanning both columns above the 21cm guide. Into this text box type 'New NHS dental centre gets go-ahead', then select the text and set its format to Arial, bold, 16 points.

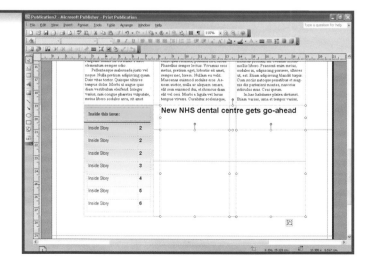

11 Right-click on the headline and select *Format Text Box*. On the *Colors and Lines* tab, click the leftmost *Presets* button to clear any existing selections, and then click the button for a top line. Change *Color* from No Line to black, and set *Weight* to 1pt. Now click on the *Text Box* tab and change *Vertical Alignment* to Middle. Click *OK*. Following the instructions in Steps 6 and 7, fill the two vertical text boxes with a few paragraphs of lorem ipsum text, then format it as you did in Step 8.

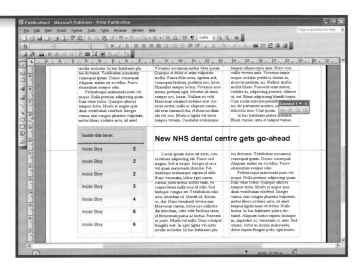

12 A useful way of adding interest to a dense section of text (or of padding out a story that's too short) is the pull quote. This is a quotation taken from the text and placed in a frame. To insert one in the NHS story, open the Design Gallery and look in the *Pull Quotes* category. Select *Waves Pull Quote* and click *Insert Object*. Position the pull quote as shown here, and change the text to 'This will move Lipton into the 21st century.' Format the text as Times New Roman, bold, 10 points, then centre it and make it black.

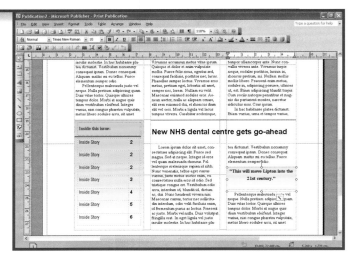

13 The blue elements in the table of contents frame now look out of place. Select the 'Inside this issue' text and use the formatting toolbar to change it to black. Then select the blue line, right-click on it and choose *Format AutoShape*. Change its colour to black and click *OK*.

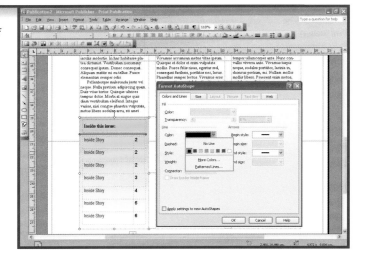

14

To insert a picture into the main story, click the Picture Frame icon in the left-hand toolbar, then select Picture from File. Drag out a frame spanning the centre column and starting at its top. When the Insert Picture dialogue box opens, navigate to the photo on your hard disk and click the Insert button. The picture will be inserted at the position you specified, but it will need to be resized to fit the full width of the frame by dragging its bottom corner handles.

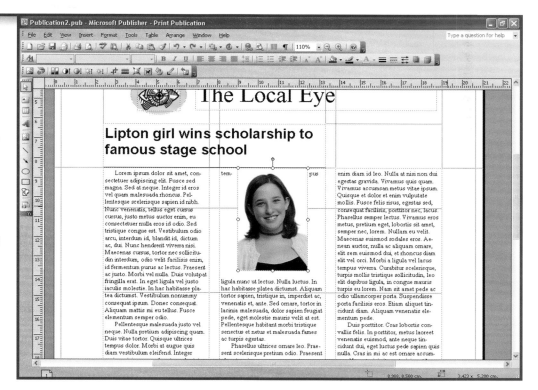

15

Draw a text box beneath the picture and insert the caption, 'Julie Carson pictured at home after hearing the news.' Format the text as Times New Roman, italic, size 9 points. It's customary to attach captions to their pictures in case you need to move them around. To do this click on the text box, then hold down Shift and click on the picture. Open the Arrange menu and click Group.

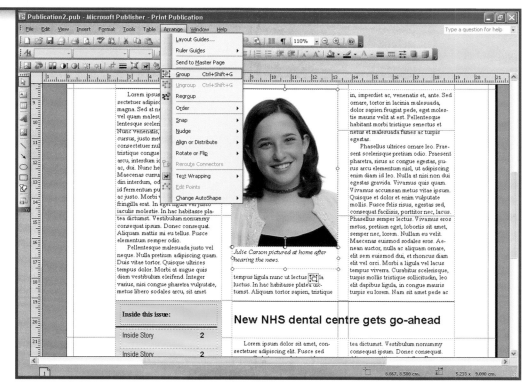

16

The final embellishment to the cover is to add decorative elements that frame the entire page and make good use of the wide margins. Switch to *Whole Page* view and then open the Design Gallery. In the *Barbells* category select *Right-Angled Barbell* and click *Insert Object*.

Design Gallery

Microsoft Office Publisher Design Gallery

Objects by Category | Objects by Design | My Objects

Categories
- Mastheads
- Tables of Contents
- Reply Forms
- Sidebars
- Pull Quotes
- Picture Captions
- Phone Tear-Off
- Calendars
- Logos
- Advertisements
- Coupons
- Attention Getters
- Barbells
- Boxes
- Checkerboards
- Dots
- Accessory Bar
- Accent Box
- Borders
- Linear Accent
- Marquee
- Punctuation

Barbells

Balanced Barbell | Right-Angled Barbell | Weighted End Barbell

Insert Object | Close

17

Position the barbell in the top left corner of the page and pull out its ends to the 16cm and 26cm ruler marks. Keep the top and side gaps between the barbell and the printed page roughly equal. Press Ctrl+C to copy the barbell, then Ctrl+V to paste a duplicate. Grab the green rotation handle of the duplicate and swing it through 180 degrees. Position the duplicate in the bottom right corner.

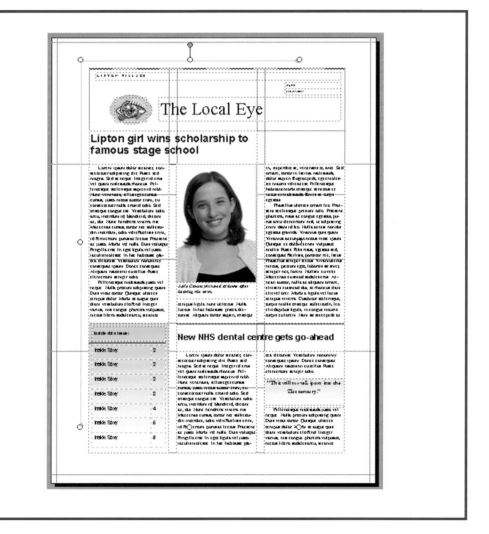

18

To add page numbers to the newsletter, open the View menu and click Master Page. On the Insert menu, click Page Numbers. Set Position to Bottom of page and Alignment to Center. Remove the tick from Show page number on first page. Click OK. Click Close Master View on the Edit Master Pages toolbar.

19

The cover page is now finished, and you're ready to go on adding and editing additional pages until the publication is complete. Adding pages is easy: just open the Insert menu and click Page, then in the Insert Page dialogue box type the number of pages required before pressing OK. When you've finished all the inside pages, return to the cover page and edit the table of contents to show the relevant story titles and page numbers.

20

Before printing any publication which has undergone heavy editing, you should get Publisher to check it for you. To do so, open the Tools menu and click Design Checker. Potential faults are then listed in the task pane. Here we see that Design Checker has flagged the two cover stories as containing overflow text. In a real situation, you'd cut and edit the text or use the overflow elsewhere.

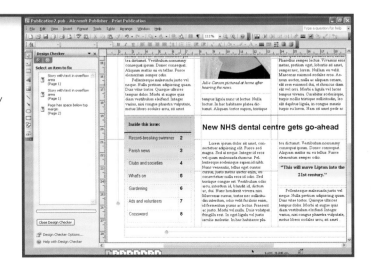

PART ③ DTP for the web

No desktop-publishing program is a match for a specialist web design program that combines interactive tools with an HTML editor and site management features. What DTP software can do is help you create a site quickly and, in the case of Microsoft Publisher, without any previous experience of website design.

You can upload your site from within Publisher via HTTP or FTP, but there are only two upload options: full or incremental. A full upload sends the entire site every time, even if most of it is already on the server, while an incremental upload sends only the files that have changed. There's no facility to remove files that have been superseded by new ones, and these will eventually use up your web space, which is why Publisher cannot be seen as a replacement for conventional web management software. For more information about producing web pages, see the *Haynes Build Your Own Website Manual.*

On the plus side, Publisher could hardly be easier to use in its convert-to-web mode. You can take any print publication and convert it for web use with a single click. Publisher will rationalise both text and graphics and, if it's a multi-page publication, add a navigation bar that points to each page. Dead simple but very basic.

A better way of using Publisher for web work is to create specifically for the web using a design template. There are four to choose from, but three of them (3-page site, Product Sales and Professional Services) are just simplifications of the fourth, which is the Easy Web Site Builder. Sites created with any of these templates can be modified for use as personal or family web pages but, as you'll see from Project 10, the templates are clearly geared towards the needs of small businesses seeking to establish an instant web presence. In the project you'll use the Easy Web Site Builder to quickly create a home page for Binnit, the fictitious recycling company we used before.

Project 10 – A simple home page

①

Start Publisher, or select New on the File menu if it is already running. In the task pane select Web sites and E-mail, then Web sites, then Easy Web Site Builder. There's the usual choice of styles in the Preview window. Because this is for Binnit, select the familiar Arrows design used in the company's print publications.

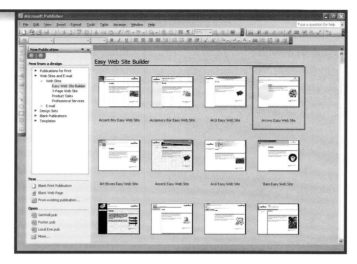

2

In this dialogue box you choose the types of pages you'd like your site to contain, and these are represented diagrammatically on the right. As you can see, because Sell products has been chosen, an icon showing multiple pages has been used, but most options generate a single page. It doesn't matter if you don't include everything at this stage because all these page types, and more, can be added later. The first three selections produce a site that is identical to what you'd have been given if you'd chosen Product Sales instead of Easy Web Site Builder. When you've selected these three, click OK.

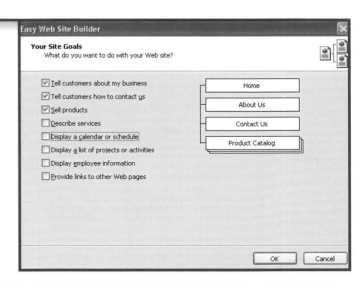

3

This is the Home page, and it contains replaceable text telling you how to use it. There is also a place-holding graphic of a running man which you can replace with something more suitable. On the left is a navigation bar pointing to three other pages: About Us, Contact Us and Product List. However, a glance at the bottom of the screen shows that there is a total of ten pages: the first is Home, the second is About Us and the third is Contact Us. Page 4 is the Product List. Click on the Page 4 icon to take a closer look.

4

Page 4 is a list of six products. For each product there's a place-holding picture you can replace with a picture of one of your own company's products, plus a description, an order number, a price and a More details link. Each of the More details links points to one of the other six pages, where full details of each product can be displayed. To see this in action, open the File menu and click Web Page Preview.

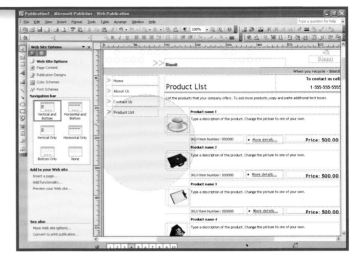

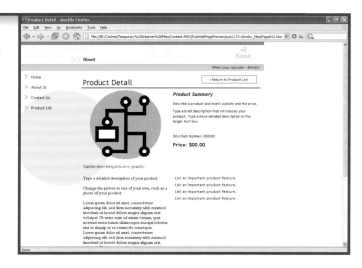

The current page opens in your usual browser (in this case Firefox), with all the links and options working just as they would if the site had already been uploaded to the web. Click on the More details link for the cup and saucer and you jump straight to Page 5 of the publication where fuller details are displayed. The place-holding picture on this page can be the same as the one on Page 4 (only bigger) or a different view of the same product. Close your browser in the usual way to return to Publisher.

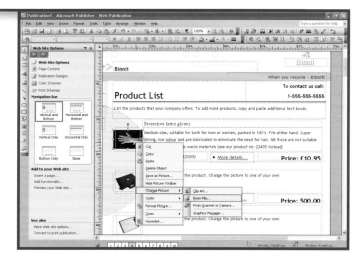

To set up the first product on Page 4, click on Product name 1 and overtype with an actual name, such as Protective latex gloves. Do the same with the description, item number and price. To replace the picture of a cup and saucer, click to select it, and then right-click and select Change Picture, followed by From File. Navigate to where a product picture is stored on disk and click Insert. You might have noted that the price on this example looks as if the numbers are too big for their text box. Don't attempt to change this: it will look fine when viewed in a browser.

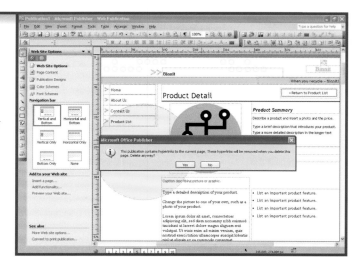

It may be that there's not much more to say about latex gloves than has already been said, so if you don't need to use the linked page for additional information you can remove the More details link by right-clicking it and selecting Delete Object. The linked page can also be removed by clicking the Page 5 icon, then opening the Edit menu and clicking Delete Page. You'll see a message asking you to confirm the deletion and the removal of all hyperlinks to this page. Click Yes. Note that when hyperlinks are removed, the associated hyperlink text remains in place, which is why you manually deleted the More details text box on Page 4. There's nothing more annoying to a user than clicking on a link to find that it is dead!

8

You can add a new page to your website at any position, but it's easier to keep track of what goes where if you add new pages at the end, so click on the Page 9 icon to go there. In the task pane are two options for new pages: Add functionality and Insert a page. Choosing Add functionality takes you to the same screen you used in Step 2 to set up the site. It's better to use the Insert a page option, which offers a wider selection of page types, as shown here. Select Calendar, then Calendar with Links, then click OK.

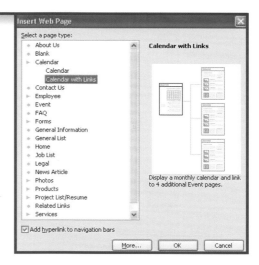

9

This simple act has produced five pages: a calendar on Page 10 and four pages linked to it on Pages 11 to 14. The Navigation bar has also sprouted a calendar option. When a calendar is created it is assigned the current month, as you'll see by going to Page 10. To change the month or the calendar style, click on the calendar and a wand appears beneath it. When you click the wand, the task pane changes to show the range of calendars available, and there's a button at the bottom to change the date.

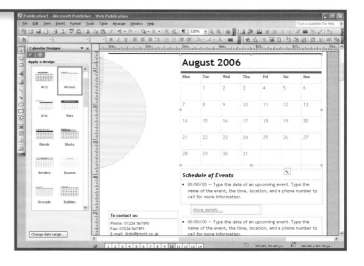

10

Later on you can experiment for yourself with other types of inserted page, but for now click the Back arrow in the task pane to return to Web Site Options. The Navigation bar options in the task pane determine where on the screen the navigation buttons are placed. Most designs seem to have been devised with vertical buttons in mind, so use the horizontal options with care.

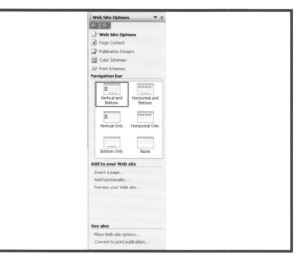

11 Click on the Page Content control near the top of the task pane for further options. There are two of interest, the first being the choice of four layouts (here we've changed to layout two, which gives more prominence to the calendar) and the other is the ability to change the background of any page and add a musical or spoken accompaniment.

12 When you click Background fill and sound, you are presented with an assortment of colours, textures and fills. If you want more, use the More colors and More backgrounds options. If you decide to add a musical or spoken background track, choose the track carefully, and limit playback to a fixed number of repeats, rather than choosing the Loop forever option. Unfortunately you cannot hear the background sound you have chosen in Publisher, even in Web Preview mode.

13 Before publishing your website, preview it in your browser. Then select Page 1, open the Tools menu and click Web page options. Under Search Engine information enter the name of your site and a description, and in the panel beneath this a list of key words separated by commas. There's a limit of 256 characters for each of these entries, so use them carefully because they help search engines to find and identify your site. At the bottom of this dialogue box is where you can decide how many times the background sound for the Home page repeats. Click OK when you've finished.

14

By default, Publisher uploads a site to its server incrementally. Because this is faster than uploading every file on every upload, it's a sensible option, but if you also want to post files to your server outside of Publisher, you may find Publisher cannot perform incremental uploads. In this case, open the Tools menu and click Options. In the Options dialogue box select the Web tab, then disable incremental publishing. Click OK.

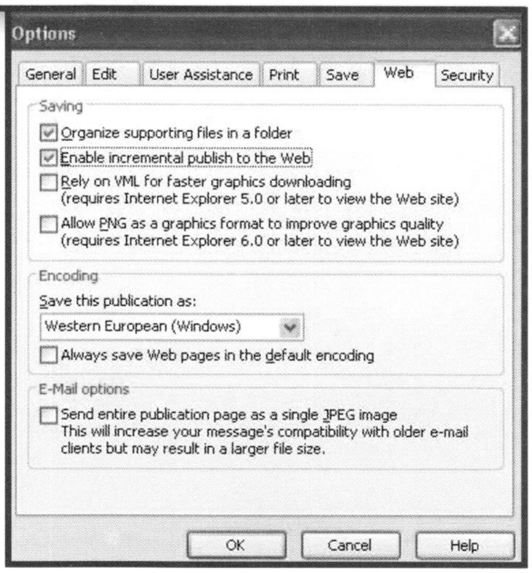

15

To upload your site to the web, select Publish to the Web. When the Publish to the Web dialogue box opens, type the HTTP address of your web space into the File name panel and click OK. This address is provided by your internet Service Provider when your web space is allocated. If your ISP says you have to upload via FTP, not HTTP, see the next step. You may also publish your website to a folder on your hard disk by navigating to the folder and saving Index.htm instead of typing an HTTP address. You may then upload the files later using a file transfer program.

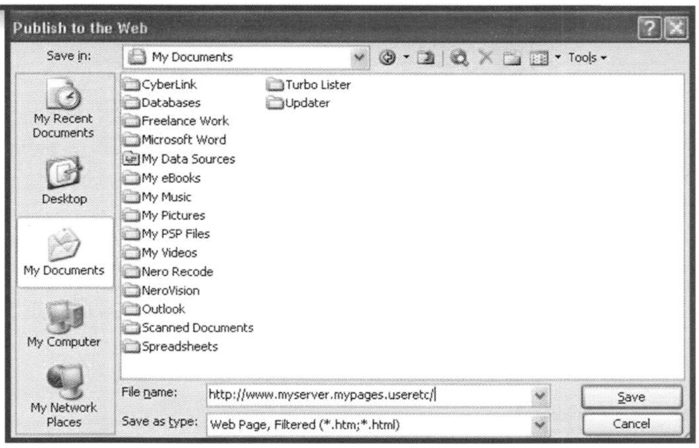

16

To publish files to an FTP server, you'll need to know the URL of the FTP server, your username and your password. In the Publish to the Web dialogue box, open the Save in panel and select Add/Modify FTP locations. In the Add/Modify dialogue box enter the server, user name and password and click Add. In the Publish to the Web dialogue box you may now select the FTP server you've just added. After logging on, a list of folders will be displayed. Navigate to the folder assigned by your ISP and click Open, then click Save.

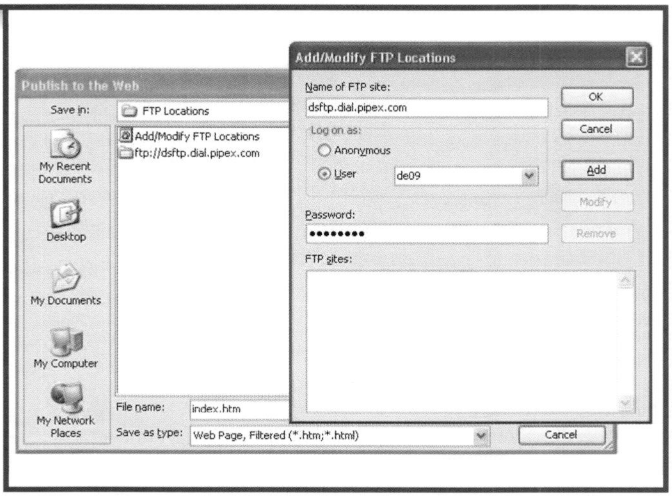

4

PART **4** **Perfect printing**

PART 4 Troubleshooting print problems

One of the most frustrating things about desktop publishing is when you print your masterpiece and it doesn't look right. Pictures that were pin-sharp on your screen look blocky and strange on the printed page, while the colour scheme that appeared so tasteful on your monitor looks like an explosion in a paint factory when it hits print. The good news is that these problems are very common – and easy to avoid.

Getting the very best results from your project isn't difficult: all you need is a little bit of inside information. Over the next few pages we'll share the secrets of perfect printing, whether you're doing it at home, using a local printing firm or dealing with online-only print shops.

Talking 'bout a resolution

If you've ever been puzzled by an image that looks great on-screen but looks bad on the printed page, the culprit is likely to be resolution. Resolution measures the quality of an image, and it's described in 'dpi'. That's short for 'dots per inch', and logically enough it tells you how many dots make up each inch of the image. The higher the number, the more dots; the more dots, the higher the quality.

One of the most common image problems that you'll find in DTP is when you take an image from the internet and print it out. The results are usually pretty bad, especially if you've made the image a bit bigger in your DTP program. That's because on-screen images usually have a much lower resolution than printed ones.

Let's take an example: you've found a great, royalty-free photo on the internet and the owner's happy for you to use it in your own project. Fantastic! So you download the image, bring it into your DTP program, come up with a suitably snazzy layout and print it off. But when you print it, the image suffers from the dreaded 'jaggies': instead of smooth curves, your images look as if they've been put together on an Etch-A-Sketch. That's because online images tend to have a resolution of 72dpi, but your printer prints at (at least) 300dpi. If everything else on your page has been printed at 300dpi, then your image will stand out for all the wrong reasons. (You'll occasionally see it in magazines and newspapers, too: while everything they do is printed at very high resolutions, occasionally somebody makes a mistake and uses a 72dpi image. That's why you'll see the odd advert that looks as if it's a photocopy of a photocopy of a photocopy.)

You can't see the difference between a 72dpi image and a 300dpi image on screen because computer monitors can't usually display more than 72dpi; the only way you'll spot the difference is if you zoom in, at which point the 72dpi image

No, it's not a printing error: this is what happens when you take a 72dpi image and zoom in on it. Because your screen displays images at 72dpi, low-quality images are only apparent when you zoom.

starts to look blocky and jaggy while the 300dpi one doesn't. You'll notice the same thing if you make the image bigger: as soon as you make a 72dpi image even slightly bigger, the quality deteriorates dramatically.

Size matters

The trick to successful image printing is to have images of sufficiently high resolution. The image resolution should be roughly double the printing output screen (measured in lines per inch, lpi). For newspapers printed with a coarse screening (70–80lpi), you can get away with an image resolution of 150–170dpi. Commercial web-offset uses a screening of 133–150lpi requiring a resolution of 300dpi. Occasionally screens of 175lpi and higher are used and these would benefit from an image resolution closer to 450dpi, although this is rare. Generally speaking the human eye won't spot any difference past 300dpi.

If you resize an image to make it smaller, you can get away with a lower resolution, but if you make the image larger then you need a higher resolution.

What does that mean? Let's say you've got an image that's 72dpi, and it's four inches wide. That means that the whole image has 288 dots from one end to the other (72dpi x 4 inches = 288 dots). If you resize that image from four inches wide to one inch wide, you still have the same amount of dots – 288 – but they're crammed into one inch, so you're effectively using an image with a resolution of 288dpi.

The numbers work in reverse, too. Let's say your image is 300dpi, and it's one inch wide: from end to end, then, you have 300 dots. If you expand that image and make it four inches wide, you're spreading those 300 dots over four times the space, so you're reducing the image resolution from 300dpi (300 dots over one inch) to just 75dpi (300 dots over four inches). The computer can't add extra dots; instead, it makes the existing dots bigger. That's why lower resolution images often look as if they're made from big blocks rather than tiny, crisp dots.

If you take a low-resolution image and make it bigger, the quality of the image deteriorates dramatically. The bigger the difference between the original size and the final size, the more obvious the deterioration.

Sensible scanning

So why do you need to know this? If you understand resolution, you can make sure your images are of high enough quality that they won't deteriorate if you resize them. So if you're using a scanner to import photographs, the first thing you need to know is the resolution at which your publication will be printed. If it's going to be 300dpi, then your finished images – the ones on the actual page – need to be 300dpi too.

To choose the scanning resolution, you also need to know how big the images will be when you print them. For example, if you want to scan an image and print it at double its original size, you'll need to double its resolution: if you're printing at 300dpi, you need to scan your image at 600dpi to keep it pin-sharp on the page. If on the other hand you're planning to make the image half its original size, then you can halve the resolution too: for printing at 300dpi, you could scan the image at 150dpi without any significant loss of quality.

We know what you're thinking: wouldn't it be sensible to scan everything at the highest possible resolution? That way it doesn't matter what you do with an image, because you'll have more than enough dots to fill every available inch. That's not a bad idea, but beware: the higher the resolution, the bigger the file, which means you'll need more disk space. Higher resolution images also need more computer memory when you're working on them, and that can slow down your computer. If you don't need to scan at 1,200dpi or higher, we'd recommend that you don't!

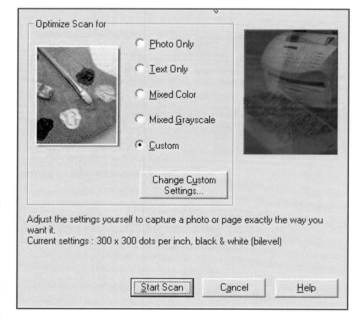

When you're scanning, think about what you're going to do with the image. If you're going to make it bigger, use the Custom options to set a higher scanning resolution.

PERFECT PRINTING

Colour me bad

If you've ever bought paint for the house, you'll know that colour can be problematic. That 'hint of lemon' turns out to be 'screaming banana' when it's on the wall; 'hint of lime' looks more like 'hospital corridor'; and 'summer red' should be renamed 'bye-bye retinas'. The colours on the chart bear as much resemblance to what's in the tin as Johnny Vegas does to Kylie Minogue, but it's not a conspiracy to make you waste money on paint: it's because accurate colour is actually quite difficult to get.

The problem isn't quite so bad with desktop publishing, but it can still drive you daft. On your screen, you've chosen a pale grey background that's barely there; on the page, it's darker than a bar of chocolate and renders your text utterly illegible. Or perhaps your Pillarbox Red prints as Shocking Pink, or your tasteful pastels have gone all day-glo. Such problems are rarely your fault, your PC's fault or your printer's fault: they're the result of a few different factors, all of which – you'll be delighted to know – are easy to address.

What you see isn't what you get

The biggest single reason for the difference between what's on screen and what's on the page is that on-screen colours work differently from printed ones. On the page, colours are made from mixing different inks together; depending on the light and on the kind of paper they're printed on, those colours will look different (try looking at some printed colour in daylight and under fluorescent light, or at colours printed on normal paper and on high-quality photo paper and you'll see what we mean). On the screen, everything you see is made from little lights, and you can change the way those lights behave by changing your monitor's brightness, contrast and other settings. Every PC user's monitor is likely to be set to suit them, and different monitors display different colours differently, too. That means no two PCs are likely to display colours the same way. What looks like a dark red on your screen might look like a very bright red on our screen, and when you print it out it may look more pink than red.

So how do you solve the problem? The first – and most important – step is to ensure that your display is correctly calibrated. This makes it much more likely that what you see on screen is what you'll get on the printed page: if you haven't done it already, zip back to Part 1 for a step-by-step guide on how to do it.

Once you've calibrated your monitor you can be confident that what you see on screen is as accurate as you can get. However, that still doesn't guarantee perfect prints – especially if you're getting your publication printed by a professional printing firm. To get the best results from professional printing, it helps if you know the different ways in which they approach colour printing.

RGB versus CMYK

Your computer displays colours using the Red, Green and Blue (RGB) model. Everything you see on-screen is made of those three colours; for example, black is 0 per cent red, 0 per cent green and 0 per cent blue, while white is 100 per cent red, 100 per cent green and 100 per cent blue. Sadly, printing firms don't work that way: they use a model called CMYK instead.

CMYK is often referred to as four-colour printing, because it uses four colours: cyan, a pale blue ink; magenta, a pinkish ink; yellow; and black (which provides the 'K' in CMYK). Combining those four different inks can create most colours (see the tint chart over the page), and you'll find that home colour printers also use CMYK . Colours printed using CMYK don't always look the same as colours created using RGB, so it's important to use CYMK colours if you're dealing with a professional printing firm.

Microsoft Publisher uses RGB by default, but it's easy to convert things to CMYK. It's a very good idea to do this before you start your publication, as it ensures you won't use the 'wrong' colours at any point.

The importance of proofs

If you've correctly calibrated your monitor and used CMYK for your colours, you should expect perfect prints. Shouldn't you? Not quite. Whenever you're dealing with a commercial printing firm you need to get a proof, which is a test print that's very, very close to what your finished job will look like. You'll often find that this looks very different from what you'd expect, and that's largely due to the limitations of CMYK.

CMYK is fine for the majority of print jobs, but it does have its limits. Some colours simply can't be created using CMYK printing. Sometimes those colours are special effects such as silvery inks, and other times they're very, very bright colours that can't be made by mixing four standard inks together. There's a way to solve that problem, though, and we'll explore it in the next section.

There's another reason to get a proof, too: for some strange reason it's very easy to miss typing mistakes on screen, but when you see the same page printed out any errors are really obvious. There's nothing worse than spending stacks of cash on a big printing job only to discover that it's full of obvious and easily corrected spelling errors, so when you get a proof don't just check the colours – have a good look at the text too.

Two-colour printing and the power of Pantone

Not everybody needs or wants four-colour printing, either because they only want a bit of colour – such as adding the odd bit of blue to a document that uses black text – or because CMYK doesn't deliver the colours they need. There's a third reason: two-colour printing is much, much cheaper than four-colour printing. It's cheaper primarily because the majority of two-colour presses are much smaller and cheaper to own and run than commercial

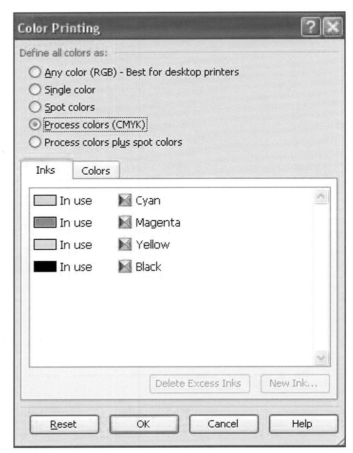

It's easy to convert colours to CMYK in Publisher: go to Tools > Commercial Printing Tools > Color Printing and choose CMYK.

four-colour presses. Factor in the savings on printing plates and set-up time and the savings are clear.

One of the most common examples of two-colour printing you'll see is on businesses' headed paper, which typically uses one colour for text and a second colour for the logo. For example, the bank First Direct uses black text with a single splash of red for the logo, while the Royal Bank of Scotland uses black and dark blue. Many newsletters also use two-colour printing, so for example the text and photos will be printed with black ink but there will be a splash of colour for the newsletter's logo or for the odd advert.

If you're preparing a publication for two-colour printing, you can still use CMYK to define the second colour. However, there's a much easier and more reliable approach, and that's to use Pantone Colour Matching.

Pantone is the industry standard for colours, and you'll find a Pantone colour chart in every self-respecting printing firm. Pantone offers colours far outside the gamut of traditional four-colour printing (including fluorescent and metallic inks) as well as single colours similar to mixes achievable with four-colour printing.

Instead of messing around with CMYK values, you can simply choose the particular colour that you want and the printer knows exactly what ink to use. There are hundreds of Pantone colours, and each one has a number: for example, the Union Jack's colours are Red 032 and Blue 286. If you were to use Red 033 and Blue 287, you'd get a very different result.

The advantage of using Pantone colours is that you know exactly what you'll get, which is why big companies use Pantone colours when they come up with their logos. For example, Pantone Blue 286 is a specific shade of blue, and you should get that shade no matter which printing firm you use, anywhere in the world. When specifying a two-colour job, use Pantone references or tell the printer that you need to print a known CMYK value as a spot colour and ask them to supply you with a Pantone equivalent.

Does Publisher support Pantone colours? It does indeed. To use Pantone colours, go to Tools > Commercial Printing Tools > Color Printing and then select Spot Colors or Process Colors. Click on the New Ink button and then choose Pantone from the Color Model drop-down.

Pantone is the industry standard for choosing colours and you can use Pantone colours from within Publisher. Your printing firm will be able to show you Pantone charts to help you pick your colours.

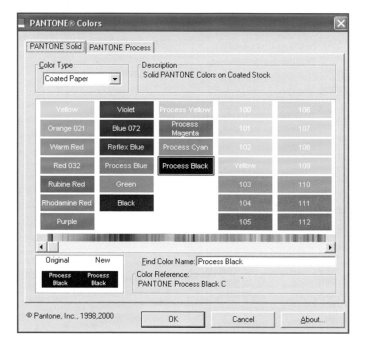

CMYK tints

To select and assess a four-colour tint, it is essential that you refer to a printed sample of that colour, preferably on paper similar to that which you will use for the job. The following charts show tints made up from cyan, magenta and yellow. They are similar to commercially available charts and are simple to use. The percentage of yellow in each chart is given in the top left corner. This amount of yellow is in every tint patch in that chart; magenta is shown along the top and cyan down the left-hand edge.

20%	0%	10%	20%	30%	40%	50%	60%	70%	80%	90%	100%
0%											
10%											
20%											
30%											
40%											
50%											
60%											
70%											
80%											
90%											
100%											

0%	0%	10%	20%	30%	40%	50%	60%	70%	80%	90%	100%
0%											
10%											
20%											
30%											
40%											
50%											
60%											
70%											
80%											
90%											
100%											

30%	0%	10%	20%	30%	40%	50%	60%	70%	80%	90%	100%
0%											
10%											
20%											
30%											
40%											
50%											
60%											
70%											
80%											
90%											
100%											

10%	0%	10%	20%	30%	40%	50%	60%	70%	80%	90%	100%
0%											
10%											
20%											
30%											
40%											
50%											
60%											
70%											
80%											
90%											
100%											

40%	0%	10%	20%	30%	40%	50%	60%	70%	80%	90%	100%
0%											
10%											
20%											
30%											
40%											
50%											
60%											
70%											
80%											
90%											
100%											

50% | 0% | 10% | 20% | 30% | 40% | 50% | 60% | 70% | 80% | 90% | 100%

0% 10% 20% 30% 40% 50% 60% 70% 80% 90% 100%

80% | 0% | 10% | 20% | 30% | 40% | 50% | 60% | 70% | 80% | 90% | 100%

0% 10% 20% 30% 40% 50% 60% 70% 80% 90% 100%

60% | 0% | 10% | 20% | 30% | 40% | 50% | 60% | 70% | 80% | 90% | 100%

0% 10% 20% 30% 40% 50% 60% 70% 80% 90% 100%

90% | 0% | 10% | 20% | 30% | 40% | 50% | 60% | 70% | 80% | 90% | 100%

0% 10% 20% 30% 40% 50% 60% 70% 80% 90% 100%

70% | 0% | 10% | 20% | 30% | 40% | 50% | 60% | 70% | 80% | 90% | 100%

0% 10% 20% 30% 40% 50% 60% 70% 80% 90% 100%

100% | 0% | 10% | 20% | 30% | 40% | 50% | 60% | 70% | 80% | 90% | 100%

0% 10% 20% 30% 40% 50% 60% 70% 80% 90% 100%

PART 4 Paper rounds

You've covered CMYK, pored over the proof and pondered Pantones. Can you expect perfect prints *now?* Er... not quite. You also need to think about paper. Choosing the right paper is essential whether you're printing at home or sending your publication to a printing firm. That's because different kinds of paper have very different properties, and if you choose the wrong type your job could end up looking awful or costing far too much money.

There are two key things you need to consider when you choose paper: its weight, and its type. The weight of paper is measured in grams per square metre (gsm) and the higher the number, the thicker the paper. Cheap inkjet paper is typically around 80gsm, while more expensive paper is 100gsm and upwards. As you'd expect thicker paper tends to look better, but it also handles ink differently: paper with a low gsm tends to be more absorbent than thicker paper, which means if you're printing with lots of ink – such as using CMYK printing – you could end up with 'bleeding'. This is when the ink spreads into other bits of ink, resulting in muddy colours and fuzzy lines.

Is inkjet paper worth the money?

If you've got an inkjet printer, you can often get away with using the very cheapest photocopy paper – the stuff that sells for pennies and doesn't come with any bright labels telling you that it's suitable for inkjets. That's fine if you want to print off the odd document for personal use, but it's not really appropriate for anything else.

Dedicated inkjet paper is less absorbent than basic photocopy paper, which means you're less likely to suffer from bleeding colours or fuzzy lines. It's only slightly more expensive than basic copy paper, too, so it won't give you a heart attack when you go to the checkout. However, such paper is best suited to jobs with fairly low ink coverage, such as text-heavy documents.

As the term suggests, ink coverage means how much of the page gets covered in ink. With a letter, report or other document, you might not even cover 5 per cent of the page with ink, so you can use pretty much any kind of paper without unhappy results. However, once you start to use photos or solid blocks of colour the coverage increases, and cheap paper can't cope.

If you've ever printed a photo onto cheap paper you'll know what we mean: the ink saturates the paper, which makes it go all wrinkly; colours often bleed into one another, and straight

lines develop furry edges. That's because the printer is spraying more ink onto the page than the paper can handle, and the results are a bit like drawing on toilet paper with a fountain pen.

Basic inkjet paper copes better than cheap copy paper, but it's still not really up to the job of printing pages that need a lot of ink coverage. For those kinds of jobs it's worth looking at specialist papers, such as glossy inkjet papers. These have two benefits over standard paper: they're thicker and they're specifically designed for high-coverage jobs such as photo printing. There's a big downside, too: they're much more expensive. For example, you can pick up 500 sheets of basic inkjet paper in your local supermarket for less than £4, but if you want photo paper you'll pay around £5 for 30 sheets. That's supermarket own-brand stuff: big-name photo-quality paper costs roughly twice that amount.

So is it worth the money? Yes and no: it depends on what you're doing. For home photo printing the answer is a firm 'yes', because high-quality inkjet paper boasts crisp, bright colours, doesn't suffer from excessive bleeding, and has been designed to resist fading. If on the other hand you want to print 100 copies of a four-page newsletter, you'll end up paying £70 just for the paper. That doesn't include the cost of ink and it assumes that every page prints perfectly.

DIY printing

There are ways to make home printing less stressful and less expensive. While the following tips can save you money, it's important to do your sums before you start a job. For anything other than modest print runs, home printing is very expensive: the paper's pricey, the ink doesn't last long and, in our experience, the bigger the job, the more likely it will go wrong. You can usually guarantee that when you do a big print job, after a while your printer will go crazy and either eat a few sheets of expensive paper, start printing things slightly squint, or run out of a particular ink colour and churn out lots of unusable pages. That's why we'd recommend you take a good look at professional printing firms, which can be much cheaper than you'd expect.

Cut the quality

Every printer is different, but you'll find that most inkjet printers enable you to specify the quality of your printouts. You'll usually find the options in the Printer Setup dialog box, and typically you can either choose the print resolution – 100dpi, 200dpi, and so on – or select between 'draft', 'normal' and 'photo' quality settings. If you're only running off a quick print to check for spelling mistakes or layout problems, use the lowest quality setting: this uses considerably less ink.

Black is the new black

Printer ink costs more per millilitre than the most expensive champagnes and perfumes, and coloured ink is much more costly than black ink. It's sensible, then, to avoid using coloured inks unless you really need to: if your printer has a separate black ink cartridge then use Printer Setup to change the print mode to Grayscale whenever you don't really need colour prints. This prints your document using only black ink instead of using all your expensive coloured inks.

Cheap isn't necessarily nasty

By all means experiment with high-quality photo papers for prints you want to pass on or keep for a long time, but if you're only printing out a web page or a draft of a publication then cheap and nasty paper will do the job just fine. The cheapest copy paper works out as a fraction of 1p per page, while premium papers can be 20p per sheet or more. It soon adds up.

Recycle rubbish prints

Don't chuck that draft printout in the bin: turn the page over and stick it back in the printer so you can use it a second time. It's better for the environment and better for your bank balance – but it only works with prints where you haven't saturated the entire sheet with ink. If you try to reuse a sheet of A4 after printing a full-page photo, you'll find that the paper is probably too warped to reuse, and is likely to cause a paper jam in your printer.

Top 'em up

Printer manufacturers don't like them, but third-party refills – either cartridges that come ready-filled, or kits that you can use to refill used cartridges at home – are widely available and are much, much cheaper than official ink cartridges.

Using refills can save you a fortune, but there are potential problems too. Refill inks might not be as fade-resistant or deliver identical colours to the manufacturers' own ink cartridges, and in the case of DIY refill kits you could well end up covered in ink. There's also a potential issue with your printer's warranty: if a third-party cartridge causes a catastrophe, the manufacturer might refuse to fix it under warranty. It's not a big risk – over the past few years we've never had a cartridge cause any serious problems beyond the odd leak – but it's still worth considering.

If you haven't tried refills before, we'd recommend you give them a go: if you like the results, you'll like the savings even more. However, while we tend to use refills for unimportant jobs – printing off shopping lists, running off quick drafts of publications and so on – we snap in official manufacturer-approved cartridges whenever we're printing something that's going to be read or looked at by other people.

PART ④ Commercial printing

When you approach a professional printing firm, they'll need several bits of information before they can tell you the price. They need to know what the job is, what type of printing you'll need, and how many copies you need.

The printer will also want to know what kind of paper you need. 80gsm matt? 120gsm gloss? 180gsm satin? There's a baffling range of papers to choose from, and it's a very good idea to pay a visit to the print shop in person so you can see what's available and even more importantly, find out the printer's opinion. A good printer won't try and persuade you to buy the most expensive paper in the shop, but he or she will be able to steer you away from bad choices such as paper that's too flimsy for the job you need it to do.

Choosing paper at the printers

Although there are thousands of different papers, they come in three key categories: matt, gloss and textured. Matt paper doesn't reflect much light and has a non-shiny appearance; it includes photocopying paper, inkjet paper and even newsprint. Gloss paper has a shiny appearance and is often used for magazines, brochures and some leaflets. Textured papers tend to be used for fancy print jobs such as business cards, letterheads, wedding invitations and product packaging. For most DTP jobs, the choice will be between a matt paper and a gloss paper.

The decision isn't as simple as 'shiny or non-shiny', although how the paper looks is obviously an important consideration. You should also consider the way your colours will appear, and how the paper looks and feels. Gloss paper tends to offer brighter, sharper colours than matt paper, but text printed on glossy paper is often harder to read than text printed on matt paper – especially in artificial light. That's why magazines typically have glossy covers but use a more matte paper for the inside pages. Glossy paper also shows up fingerprints, and while you can often get away with a lower weight of paper for gloss than for matt paper, if the paper's too thin you'll get show-through, where the back of the page is visible when you're looking at the front.

Even when you've decided on gloss or matt paper, the decisions aren't over: you then need to choose the weight of the paper – 80gsm? 120gsm? more? – and then choose a specific kind of paper. For example, there's no such thing as a standard gloss paper; instead, there are different kinds of gloss available from different firms. Some firms' paper is whiter than others'; some firms' paper is cheaper; some firm's paper is shinier; some firms' paper is more environmentally friendly. Once again, it's a big help if you can talk to an expert printer about these things, as his or her product knowledge is invaluable.

While you're talking to your printer, find out what formats they can accept work in. If they can accept Microsoft Publisher files – many do – then things will be nice and easy, but if they don't you'll need to find out what other formats they can accept. The most likely alternative will be PostScript, which is widely used in the printing industry and which you can create from within Publisher.

Preparing Publisher files for the print shop

The easiest way to get your publication ready is to use Publisher's Pack and Go Wizard, but before you do that you need to consider three things: page size, fonts and bleeds.

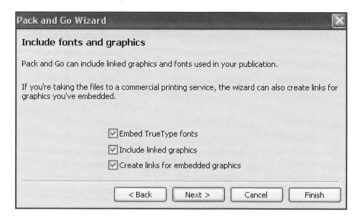

It's a good idea to ensure that the page size in Publisher is the same page size you want printed, so if it's an A4 document then your page size should be A4 too. Don't assume that's the case: many Windows programs default to the American Letter page size instead of A4, so it's worth checking. If your printed documents will be bigger than A4, make sure that's the case in your Publisher project too: that way the printer won't have to resize anything to make it bigger, which could mean a drop in quality.

Publisher takes its page sizes from the printer that's attached to your system, so for really big page sizes you might find that Publisher won't let you specify huge pages. To get round this, go to File > Page Setup and click on the Properties button next to the name of your printer. You can now adjust the page width and height to the correct sizes.

If you're using the Pack and Go Wizard, make sure you've ticked the box to embed fonts and graphics. That means your Publisher file will include all the images and fonts you've used in your project; don't assume that the printing firm has the same fonts that you do or you could end up with a nasty surprise when you see the proofs.

If colours reach the very edge of your pages, you'll also need to allow a 'bleed'. This means making the coloured areas bigger than the finished page so that the printer can print colours right to the margin. The extra bits are chopped off, giving perfect colour to the very edge of your page.

Adding a bleed is simple enough: ask the printing firm how much bleed they need, and adjust the coloured bits of your document accordingly. For example if your pages are A4 (21cm by 29.7cm) and the printing firm needs a 5mm bleed, simply drag the coloured areas so they exceed the page edge by 5mm. Unless the printing firm asks otherwise, leave everything else where it is!

You're nearly ready to export your publication, but there's one final step. From the Tools menu, select Design Checker. This double-checks your document for any problems, such as text boxes that have been cut off prematurely or items that overlap. It only takes a few seconds to run the Design Checker, but it can save a lot of heartache later on!

Once you've followed these steps, you can now export your publication and either burn it to CD, upload it to the internet or e-mail it to your print firm. If you're planning to e-mail it, check the file size – if it's more than 1MB in size, it's probably too big to e-mail. Many printing firms have an FTP (short for File Transfer Protocol) server you can use to upload your files if they're too big to e-mail; give the firm a call to find out where it is and what username and password you need to use.

There's a useful commercial printing checklist on the Microsoft Publisher website at **http://office.microsoft.com/en-us/assistance/HP030746221033.aspx**, and you'll find lots of links to commercial printing advice on the All Graphic Design website at **www.allgraphicdesign.com/preflightchecklist.html**.

If you can't find a local print shop that is able to work with Pack and Go Publisher files, you can send them to an online print shop. Microsoft maintains a web page at **http://mspublisher.saltmine.com/printerSearch.aspx**, where you can search for online print shops in different countries. At the time of writing, there are 13 Publisher-capable online print shops in the UK.

Preparing PostScript files for the print shop

If you'd rather use a local printer who can hold your hand and offer help and advice, then it's up to you to convert your Publisher files into a format that the print shop can work with. The required format is PostScript, from which the print shop can generate PDF files by a process called distillation. The distilled PDF files are suitable for outputting to commercial printing equipment.

Because PostScript files can be assembled in different ways, and the method used affects the way they must subsequently be distilled and printed, it's important to talk to your printer beforehand and find out which system is preferred. In particular, you'll need to know whether your printer requires colour separations or a composite PostScript file, and you might also be given instructions about other issues including how colours should be handled, which printer's marks are required, and whether you need to produce standard or page-independent PostScript files. You don't need to understand the intricacies of these options because they are selected simply by ticking boxes during the file-making process. In the absence of instructions to the contrary, you can use Publisher's default settings.

Armed with this information you're ready to produce PostScript files following the step-by-step guidelines below.

1

Before you can create PostScript files, you need to install a PostScript printer driver on your computer. If your desktop printer is of the PostScript type you'll already have one, but if not you'll need to install the generic PostScript driver supplied with Microsoft Publisher. To do this in Windows XP, click on the Start Menu button and select Control Panel. Click Printers and other Hardware, and then click Add a Printer.

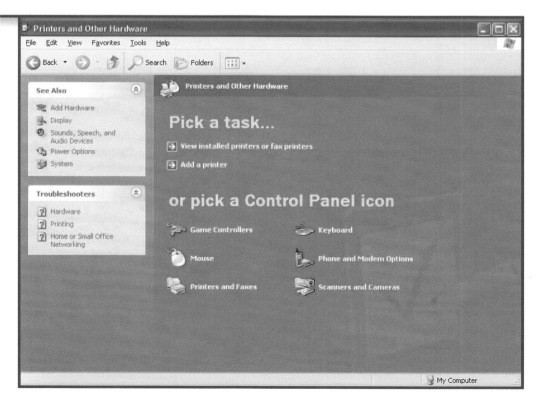

②

When the Add Printer wizard appears, click Next. Ensure that the option 'Local Printer attached to this Computer' is selected but be sure to deselect the option to automatically detect and install a plug and play printer. Click Next. When asked to select a printer port, accept the default selection of LPT1 and click Next. On the wizard screen shown here, ignore the printer selection lists and click the Have Disk button instead.

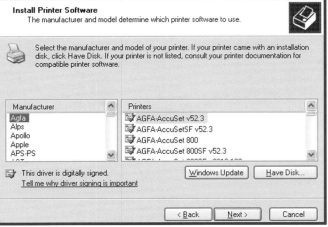

③

In the Install from Disk dialogue box, click the Browse button and navigate to the Program Files folder of the hard disk where Publisher is installed (this is usually drive C:). Double-click the Microsoft Office folder and then double-click the Office 11 folder. Finally, double-click the file called MSCOL11.INF. This returns you to the Install from Disk dialogue box, where you should click OK. Back at the Add Printer wizard, you'll see that Generic Color PS for Commercial Printing is ready for installation. Click Next, and keep clicking Next until you arrive at the Print Test page. Select No when the wizard offers to print a test page, then click Next. To close the wizard, click Finish.

④

Steps 1 to 3 need only be performed the first time you create PostScript files. Thereafter you can begin here. Start by opening the publication you wish to convert in Publisher. If you have been requested to create a page-independent PostScript file (one in which the pages can be rearranged and printed selectively) jump to Step 7. Otherwise, open the File menu and click Print. In the Print dialogue box, select Generic Color PS for Commercial Printing.

5

Click the Advanced Print Settings button in the bottom left corner of the Print dialogue box. On the Separations tab, use the drop-down Output list to select Composite CMYK or Separations, according to your printer's advice. If Composite CMYK is selected, that's all there is to it, but if Separations are required, there are further options available to you. The default settings are fine for most purposes, but if your printer has advised you to convert spot colours to process or specified a customised halftone screen, make the appropriate changes here. If you have been given explicit instructions about bleeds and printer's marks, click the Page Settings tab and make the appropriate selections, then click OK.

6

Back in the Print dialogue box, tick the Print to file box. Click OK, then in the Print to File dialogue box navigate to the folder where you'd like to save the PostScript files. Type a file name (which is normally the same as the publication name) and add the extension .PS after the filename to ensure that the resulting output is identified as a PostScript file. A single file with the designated name is saved on disk. It contains all the information a print shop requires to distil a PDF file for printing.

7

If page-independent output is required, open the File menu and select Save As. Navigate to the folder where you'd like the PostScript files to be stored, then in the Save as type panel select PostScript, and click Save. When the Save as PostScript File dialogue box is displayed, click Properties. On the Layout tab, click the Advanced button to display the Advanced Document settings shown here. Click the plus sign next to PostScript Options to expand the options. Click PostScript Output Option and in the drop-down list change Optimize for Speed to Optimize for Portability.

Click OK twice to return to the Save as PostScript File dialogue box. Click the Advanced Print Settings button and follow the advice given in Step 5 regarding the options available for separations and page settings. When you've done, click the Save button to generate the PostScript output in the designated folder. The single file contains all the information a print shop requires to distil a PDF file for printing.

Save As PostScript File

Create a PostScript file named SkiScene.ps in:
D:\My Documents\

Printer

Name: Generic Color PS for Commercial Printing ▼ [Properties...]

Type: Generic Color PS for Commercial Printing

[Advanced Print Settings...]   [Save]   [Cancel]

Using online print shops

Throughout this chapter we've concentrated on local printing firms, the sort of places you'll find in the *Yellow Pages* or local paper. However, there's a growing number of online printing firms who can accept orders over the internet without ever meeting you. There are pros and cons to such firms: they're often – but not always – cheaper than 'real-world' print firms, but you don't get the face-to-face contact that you get when you deal with a local firm. If you could do with the help and support of a local firm then it's perhaps a good idea to leave the online print shops until you feel a bit more confident.

Online print shops such as Printing Direct (**www.printingdirect.com**) enable you to upload your files and get your finished prints delivered a few days later. They can be much cheaper than traditional printing firms, but of course you can't pop in for a bit of advice and a cup of tea.

PART **④** Commercial printing: the seven deadly DTP sins

We spoke to some commercial printing firms to find out if there are mistakes that DTP users often make, and it seems that the same errors happen everywhere. These are the seven deadly sins of DTP:

Colour catastrophes

Many people don't realise the difference between RGB and CMYK, or between RGB colours and Pantone colours, and using the wrong colour model can cause problems at the print shop (see p.130.). Always make sure your files use the right kind of colours for the print job, and that your monitor has been calibrated for accurate colours (see p.33.).

Forgotten fonts

Just because a font is on your computer doesn't mean it's on the printing firm's computer – and if it isn't, their machine will usually come up with its own suggested font. Standard Windows fonts – Arial, Times New Roman and so on – are on every machine, but if you use more obscure fonts then make sure they're included with the files you send to the printing firm.

Missing links

By default, Publisher includes all images in the files it creates using the Pack and Go Wizard, but it's possible to turn that feature off. The easiest way to check that things will work on someone else's machine is to try loading your publication from CD (or an external storage device – hard disk, USB pen drive, whatever's handy) rather than from the hard disk. If the images appear, then everything's fine. If they don't, you'll need to go back and re-export your files with the images embedded.

Poor pictures

As we explained earlier, images grabbed from the internet are often very low quality and look awful when they're on the printed page – especially when they're resized. Make sure your images have the correct resolution for print rather than for on-screen viewing (see p.126.).

Unchecked output

Make sure your project is perfect before you send it to the printer, and print off a version at home so you can squash any typing mistakes, layout errors or other nasties. The second worst time to try and fix problems is when you're paying the printer to do it; the worst time, of course, is after the job has been printed.

Wrong formats

It's easy to find out what file formats a printing firm can and can't read: if they have a website, they'll probably list them on the site; if they don't, it only takes a few seconds to phone up and ask. There's no point submitting a file in Publisher format if the print firm can only read PostScript files: all that does is waste time!

And the worst sin of all?

Not asking questions

If in doubt, ask! If you're not sure what you want, then the printing firm's in the dark too – so they're much less likely to spot any potential problems. Printers are experts in everything to do with ink and paper, so if you're unsure about any part of the process from choosing the right paper to submitting your project electronically, then ask. Don't learn the hard way.

5

PART 5 **Appendices**

Appendix 1 – Design tips

The website **http://webpagesthatsuck.com** promises to 'teach good design by showing bad design', and it's very effective: once you've seen the horrors that lurk within, you'll never make the same mistakes yourself. It's an approach that works with DTP too. One of the best ways to appreciate good design is to see some vivid examples of how not to do it, and of course to find out why the design doesn't work. Prepare yourself: over the next few pages we'll look closely at some real DTP disasters, which you'll soon notice everywhere you look.

Font frenzies

> **Just** because **there** ARE **400 fonts** on your PC DOESN'T mean YOU have to **use** all of **them!**

By far the most common DTP disaster is to go mad with fonts: look on any public noticeboard and you'll see at least one poster where someone has tried to put every single font ever created on a single sheet of A4. The only time using lots of different fonts is acceptable is if you're putting together a catalogue of fonts; for the overwhelming majority of desktop publishing, try to use one or two. With fonts, two is the magic number: use one for headlines and one for body text. If you look at any decent bit of design from newspapers and magazines to posters and packaging, professional designers tend to stick to one font for headlines and another one for body text.

Traditional wisdom suggests body copy should be set in a serif font like Times New Roman or Garamond. This is because the addition of serifs (the little sticky-out bits) to font characters can help guide the readers eye from one letter to the next, especially at the smaller sizes associated with large quantites of text. This is not the only option, however. It is increasingly common to find

Serif fonts have little additions to the letter forms that help to visually join letters together and aid reading, especially at smaller sizes.

Sans-serif fonts offer a crisp clean alternative to serif fonts and have traditionally found their place in headlines and display headings. Current trends see sans-serif fonts increasingly used for body copy.

Butch Butch

Butch

Be careful that your choice of font is appropriate and doesn't say the wrong thing about you or your company.

sans-serif fonts being used for body copy and, if used carefully, this is fine. For an example you need look no further than this very book (set in News Gothic Light).

An interesting exercise is to choose a single font – say, Arial – and use only that font in your publication. There's a surprising amount of variation available: you can make it bold or italic, stretch it or compress it, put it in different colours and so on. With so many choices available from a single font, do you really need to introduce another one?

If you do intend using two different fonts, try to select one serif and one sans-serif rather than two of the same kind.

Another common font failure is the use of fonts in the wrong places, or in the wrong way. For example, we've seen business communications printed in curly, girlie fonts, which is fine for a curly, girlie business but not so good if you're selling bricks to burly builders. Watch out for striking-looking fonts, too: many of them are completely unreadable in smaller sizes.

Slipshod spelling

GET YOU'RE FREE PIZZA'S!!!!

This is the second most common DTP disaster, and it's utterly avoidable. However, don't rely on a spell-checker to catch everything: many spell-checkers won't differentiate between 'its' and 'it's', 'there' and 'their', 'ours' and 'hours', and they might not spot dodgy punctuation such as 'voucher's' when you mean 'vouchers'. Murphy's law means the most appalling mistakes will always appear somewhere obvious, such as in a headline or on the front page.

Clip-art craziness

They say a picture speaks a thousand words, which is true – but a bad picture speaks a thousand bad words, and you don't want that.

Almost every DTP program on the planet comes with a selection of clip art, and you should avoid using it if at all possible. The problem with clip art is that much of it is very low quality, and because different programs tend to provide the same clip art you'll see the same images again and again and again. Oh look – it's an office worker surrounded by paper, waving a white flag! Noooooo!

Pictures are important, and not all clip art is bad. However, a photo is much more attractive and effective, and if you must use clip art try to avoid anything that's clichéd. If people have seen an image again and again, it loses any impact it might once have had, so there's little point in using it.

Clip-art may seem like an attractive option to save time and money. For maps, flags and other general symbols this can often prove to be the case, illustrations like these should be avoided though.

Crushed copy

There's a saying in the advertising industry: white space sells. The more cramped a page appears, the less attractive it is – which means people are less likely to read it.

Cramped pages are usually due to one of two reasons: there's either far too much text or the text size is too big. If it's the latter, reducing the font size and increasing the line spacing can make the page look much less intimidating. You could also try newspaper tricks such as drop capitals or pull-quotes to make your text more attractive.

If the problem is that you're trying to cram too much text into your publication, the answer's simple: get rid of some of the text. No matter how well written the text might be, you can almost always make it better by making it shorter. It's particularly important if you're putting together a flyer, a poster or an advert: you need to attract people's attention immediately or they'll read something else. Don't use three paragraphs if three words will say the same thing more effectively.

In the example above the problem is compounded by the use of fully justified text, which can look heavy and slab-like on the page. Justified text can also prove difficult to format without introducing uneven spaces between words, especially if your column width is too narrow. Hyphenation can help rectify these untidy spaces, but some people find the way words break onto the next line difficult to read.

To be honest, you can do a lot worse than stick with left-aligned text as used in this book. Most people find it to be the easiest text formatting to read.

You should avoid the use of right-aligned text for longer passages of text as the ragged left edge can make it difficult to read onto the next line of text, although it is perfectly readable in shorter lengths like captions in magazines and can help balance a design.

It is best to stick with one style of formatting to avoid confusion. If your body text is justified, make sure it stays consistent throughout the design. You can always left-align headings or right-align pull-quotes to liven up the layout.

The Day The Music Died

Think you own your record collection, or your books, or any other media? Think again.

[Sample magazine page shown in justified columns, used as an illustration of cramped, fully-justified text.]

It's been a long day, and you deserve a treat. Maybe that reissue of the Jeff Buckley album, or the new U2 one. You make a detour on the way home to stop at the record shop, but it's boarded up – it looks like it's gone bust.

Left-aligned text is neat and easy to read.

It's been a long day, and you deserve a treat. Maybe that reissue of the Jeff Buckley album, or the new U2 one. You make a detour on the way home to stop at the record shop, but it's boarded up – it looks like it's gone bust.

Right-aligned text is can be hard to follow.

It's been a long day, and you deserve a treat. Maybe that reissue of the Jeff Buckley album, or the new U2 one. You make a detour on the way home to stop at the record ▯ shop, ▯ but ▯ it's boarded up – it looks like it's gone bust.

Justified text has well-defined edges but is prone to untidy spaces between words like line seven in the example above.

It's been a long day, and you deserve a treat. Maybe that reissue of the Jeff Buckley album, or the new U2 one. You make a detour on the way home to stop at the record shop, but it's boarded up – it looks like it's gone bust.

Hypenation can help tidy up awkward spaces in text. By hyphenating the word *boarded* we can remove the problem seen in the previous example.

Missing the point

Have you ever been stuck at traffic lights, glanced at a poster and been unable to read it because it used tiny text? You've just spotted a designer who's missed the point. With good design, form follows function, so newspaper-style columns of text won't work on a poster, tiny text is pointless on a roadside advertisement and using microscopic text in an advertisement for reading glasses is a spectacular own goal.

Incorrect emphasis

Some posters and flyers suffer from incorrect emphasis, where the design draws attention to the wrong things. For example, we received a flyer the other day from a firm whose logo dominated the page, and it wasn't immediately obvious what the flyer was supposed to be promoting. With publicity materials of any kind, their purpose is to get a message across – so the message should be the very first thing anybody sees on the page. In the design world this is referred to as hierarchy, or reading order.

Before you even put pen to paper, you need to decide the order in which the information should be read.

A poster, for instance, should tell the reader what it is promoting, followed by when the event takes place so a reader can decide if they're interested and available. Where it is and why it should be of interest to them is less significant.

There are many ways to control reading order in your designs:

- You may choose to vary the size of the text to place emphasis on a specific word or sentence.
- Varying the weight of font (bold, medium or light) can influence reading order and this is often used in combination with size variations.
- Text colour, used where appropriate, can have a huge influence on the order in which elements on a page attract our attention, just remember that warm colours, like red, orange, yellow and magenta, tend to stand out from the page where as green, blue and purple offer less impact and are perceived to receed into the page.
- Italics can be used to emphasise certain words, though this usually happens within body copy.

This ficticious poster promoting a local music festival demonstrates how colour and variations in the choice of font weight can influence the order in which a reader absorbs information.

Study the examples below, then ask yourself which words drew your attention first.

You can **control** the reading order in many different ways	You can control the **reading order** in many different ways	You can control the reading order in many **different** ways	You can control the reading order in many different ways

Chaotic colour

Used correctly, colour adds impact. Used badly, it hurts your eyes and can make your publication illegible. It's tempting to use a different colour for each letter in a headline, but it usually looks terrible; similarly while it's possible to print body text in lime green on a bright yellow background, it's rarely a good idea.

It is also worth bearing in mind that some colours have strong associations. Bright pink headings might seem like a great way draw a readers attention but would probably be considered poor form in a publication aimed at mechanics. Classic deep reds and blues imply authority and taste, where as bright blue or orange would be considered more youthful and fun.

The best approach is to limit your colour palette to two complementary colours. By setting rules for what what you can and cannot do, you'll find more creative solutions for your designs. With colour – as with most design elements – less is more.

When looking for colour combinations that work well together, you should start by selecting opposing colours from the colour wheel shown right.

If you intend to use one colour for text and one for the background, it might be worth considering a tint for the second colour to aid legibility. Just watch out, not all combinations look good together.

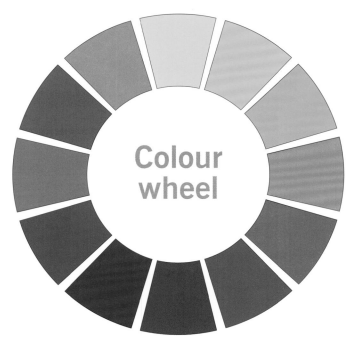

Colour wheel

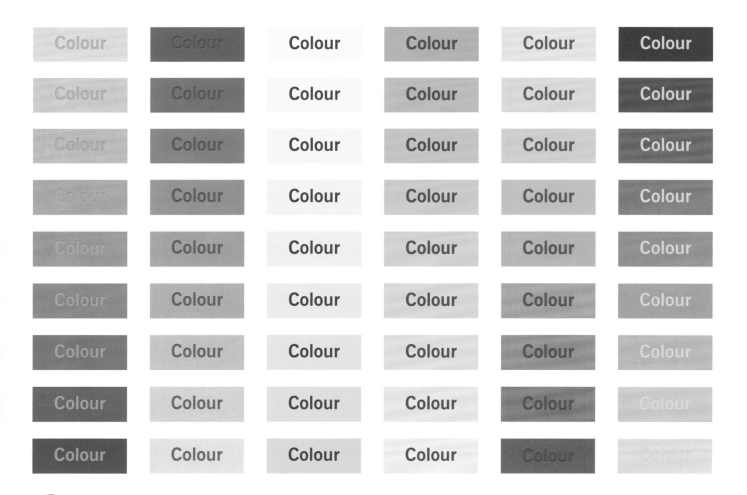

Text and image

DTP software allows you to layer text elements on top of other parts of your design, such as photographs or textures. Done well this can be a great way to add a distinctive and unique look to your design. Done badly it can seriously jeopardise the readability of your work.

There are some useful guidelines to follow if you are considering running text over the top of an image:

- Try to avoid heavily textured backgrounds and or textures with too much contrast (strong dark areas and light areas).
- If you intend to run body copy over an image consider increasing the weight of font used in your body copy.
- Always look for plain areas of the image to use for text and consider this when selecting images (blue sky makes for a great background – clouds less so)
- Be careful when choosing colours for text. Where possible try to stick with black on lighter areas and white on darker areas, but don't mix black and white words together – pick one and stick with it.

Amazing acronyms

Acronyms – words made from the initials of other words, such as NASA (National Aeronautics and Space Administration), RAF (Royal Air Force) or AIDS (Acquired Immune Deficiency Syndrome) – can be useful if you want to get a big message across in a little space, but sometimes it's obvious that the designer of a poster or flyer couldn't think of a decent headline and decided to go with a bad acronym instead. Don't do it!

This is a real example – can you guess what it spells?

Good health lasts a lifetime so screening can give you the opportunity to be a well person

According to a Scottish hospital, that little spiel becomes GLASGOW – when in fact it really should be GHLALSSCGYTOTBAWP. Here's how they did it:

Good health **L**asts **A** lifetime so **S**creening can **G**ive you the **O**pportunity to be a **W**ell person

The poster was supposed to make us think about our health, but instead it made us wonder about the designer's mental health – which means the design was a complete failure.

Bad boxes

Boxes are handy things. Newspapers use them to add related information to main stories; magazines use them to provide extra snippets of information or comedy; and in business publications, they're a good way to separate stories and make a page look more attractive. However, the secret of success is to use them in moderation. One or two boxes on a page will work, but if you've got 12 then the page will just look messy.

Another common mistake with boxes is to use a bad background colour, such as a vivid red or yellow. Black text looks hideous over such colours, and white text is often illegible; even worse, such a vivid colour completely dominates the page. Greys can be tricky, too: a very pale grey is fine underneath black text, but if the grey is too dark your text will disappear.

You're liable to run into trouble if you don't follow our simple guidelines, or if you ask too much of your reader.

Appendix 2 – Successful DTP in practice

Thanks to affordable PCs and ever-smarter desktop-publishing software, anyone can create professional-looking publications without having to spend huge sums of cash. The technology has been embraced by all kinds of businesses from one-man bands to giant corporations. While the businesses differ their use of DTP tends to be for very similar reasons: it's fast, it's flexible, and most importantly of all, it saves them a fortune. Over the next few pages, we'll discover how four very different firms use desktop-publishing software to tell the world about what they do.

Case study 1: Scoopt

When photo agency Scoopt launched in July 2005, its marketing budget suffered from a little problem: there wasn't enough money in the kitty to have a marketing budget. Undeterred, the firm used a clever combination of desktop publishing and word-of-mouth marketing to spread the word about Scoopt. Rather than print off thousands of flyers, Scoopt designed a poster in Publisher but stuck it on its website instead of printing any copies. Scoopt members then downloaded the poster, printed it off and put it up around their home towns.

Why would people print and publicise a firm they didn't work for? Scoopt's secret weapon was a referral scheme. If a member persuaded others to join, that member would get a cut of any photo sales from the new member – so the more people you recruited, the more likely you were to make money. It was a very smart move that ensured that the name of Scoopt swiftly spread far and wide – by which time the firm had made enough cash to start paying for newspaper adverts, which once again it designed in Publisher.

In addition to creating their own publicity materials such as flyers and brochures, Scoopt also uses DTP to design their newspaper adverts. That way, they know exactly what will appear in print.

Although DTP is usually used for print publications, there's no reason why you can't also publish your documents online. Scoopt saved this poster as a PDF file and put it on its website for members to download and print at home.

Case study 2: Helena Stirling

The world of hair and beauty is a fiercely competitive one, particularly when – like Helena Stirling – your premises are on the first floor of a busy High Street that contains several rival salons. As director Christine Howat explains, 'You can't just put a sign in the window and wait for people to come in – particularly when you're not at street level.' 'You need to make people aware of who you are and what you do, or they'll walk right past and go into one of your competitors instead. We can't have that!' she laughs. When the salon opened last year, the firm used DTP software to put together a range of items including money-off vouchers, price lists and publicity flyers, all of which were handed out to passers-by. The firm still designs and distributes flyers, and it puts together its own brochures in-house too.

'We don't do everything in-house,' Christine explains. 'We paid a professional illustrator to come up with our logo – we tried a few designs ourselves, but we didn't like them so we decided to call in an expert. We use external printing firms too, so whenever we want to do colour brochures or colour flyers we give them a call – it's too expensive to do colour printing in-house. But most of the documents we need to create are simple, so it's quicker and cheaper to do it ourselves.'

One of the big advantages of DTP is speed: if the staff at Helena Stirling decide to change their flyers, they can simply load up the original and make the necessary changes in seconds.

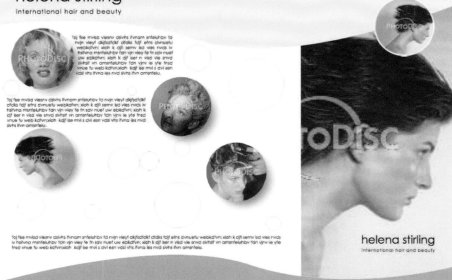

Not all of Helena Stirling's marketing material is printed in-house. This draft version of a flyer was designed in-house, but once the library images were bought, it was then e-mailed to a printing firm to get the brochures professionally printed.

Case study 3: Kelvin Timber

Kelvin Timber sells building materials ranging from soft- and hardwoods to bricks, cement, decking and DIY supplies. With a huge range of products and prices that change regularly, the firm's copy of Microsoft Publisher comes in very handy: price lists can be updated and printed off in seconds, product lists can be adapted to deal with shortages or surpluses, and the firm can easily dash off a few flyers to promote special offers in its shop. As managing director, Frank McHugh, explains, 'Because we do everything in-house we can put things together very quickly and cheaply so, for example, if we've got a special offer on a particular product, we can have posters up within a few minutes.' It saves money, too. 'Prices change a lot in our industry, sometimes on a weekly basis,' Frank says. 'If we were getting price lists professionally printed, we'd end up with lots of unused bits of paper whenever our suppliers changed their prices. By doing it in-house we just run off as many as we need, so there's no waste.'

Building firm Kelvin Timber uses desktop publishing to put together brochures, price lists and posters in-house.

Case study 4: Haynes Publishing – marketing

While the designers at Haynes are busy producing books, covers, brochures, advertising and exhibition material – using Quark and Indesign on Mac computers, the marketing department are busy producing most of their work using Microsoft Publisher. This includes over 200 different press releases each year for all new titles, along with point-of-sale literature. Chris Wall, our marketing executive, said that even though Word is capable of producing a certain standard of document, Publisher gives them much more scope with the design and layout elements.

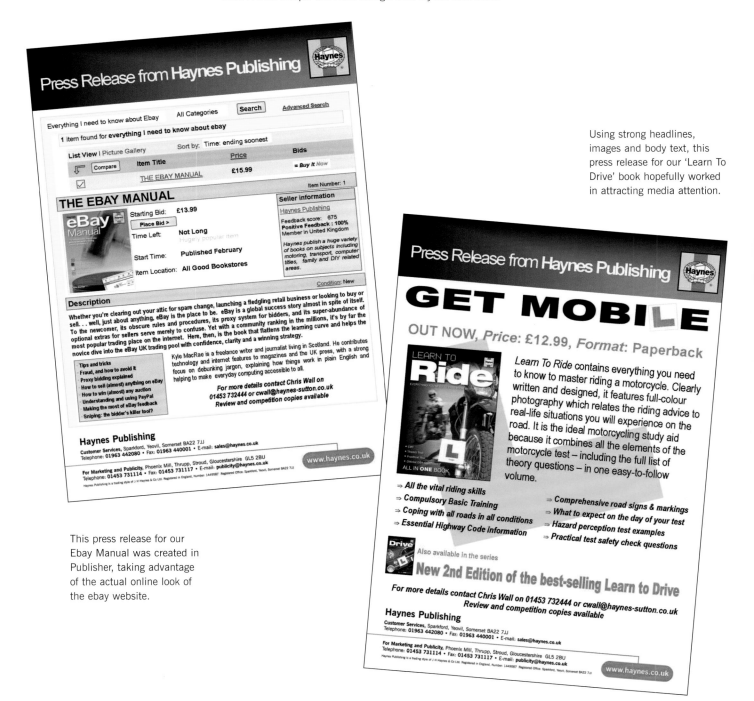

Using strong headlines, images and body text, this press release for our 'Learn To Drive' book hopefully worked in attracting media attention.

This press release for our Ebay Manual was created in Publisher, taking advantage of the actual online look of the ebay website.

PART **5** Index

Acknowledgements:
Grateful thanks to Gary Marshall and Paul Wardley

Author	**Kyle MacRae**
Copy Editor	**Shena Deuchars**
Page build	**James Robertson**
Index	**Nigel d'Auvergne**
Project Manager	**Louise McIntyre**